Mother Earth's hassle-free VEGETABLE COOKBOOK

by Joel Rapp
illustrations by
Marvin Rubin

AVON
PUBLISHERS OF BARD, CAMELOT AND DISCUS BOOKS

MOTHER EARTH'S HASSLE-FREE VEGETABLE COOKBOOK is an original publication of Avon Books. This work has never before appeared in book form.

AVON BOOKS
A division of
The Hearst Corporation
959 Eighth Avenue
New York, New York 10019

Published by arrangement with the author
Library of Congress Card Number: 80-69611
ISBN: 0-380-76851-8

Cover design by Marc J. Cohen
Author's photograph by Richard Brenner

First Avon Printing, April, 1981

Printed in the U.S.A.

This book is dedicated to my mother and Page, without whom it wouldn't have been possible; and to my beautiful daughters Lisa and Danielle, without whom it wouldn't have been necessary. And a special thanks to Madeline Oolie for all her help.

Table of Contents

Foreword

Hello.

Here I am again—Mr. Mother Earth, the World's Foremost Authority on Indoor Plants (a title bestowed upon me by a most discerning individual: my mother).

Only this time we're not going to be talking about growing plants, we're going to be talking about eating them!

Don't panic. Your ferns and philodendrons are safe. The plants we'll be talking about are the ones that were born to be eaten, namely, vegetables.

Ahh . . . I can hear you asking, "So how come the hot-shot plant man is writing a vegetable cookbook?"

Simple: So that those of you who want to start eating more meatless meals but are afraid, as I used to be, that vegetable cooking is dull, or a lesson in self-denial, or too difficult, or whatever, can be assured that it is indeed none of the above.

So you can discover, as I did, that eliminating meat from your diet, or at least cutting way down, will *not* mean the end of Epicurean feasting. *Au contraire!* You will, in fact, find you'll be eating better, enjoying it more, and spending less. In further fact, I'm sure you'll discover, as I did, that a well-planned, carefully prepared Hassle-Free vegetable diet will not only not be the end of your gourmet experience, but the beginning!

More importantly, I hope it will be the beginning of—for lack of a better phrase—"The Cooking Experience." Let me stress again that these recipes are, in varying degrees, Hassle-Free. You do not need a fully outfitted "French chef"-type kitchen to rustle them up (see "The Kitchen"). They don't cost a lot of money. And they taste good. Once you have lost your "Fear of Frying" and become convinced that cooking is at least as much fun as stamp-collecting, *then* I encourage you to return to your bookstore or library and load up on vegetable—or any other kind—of cookbooks. I hope I can get you so involved that cooking will become your life! But first things first.

In "Mother Earth's Hassle-Free Indoor Plant Book" I did not lead you down the garden path; I frankly and honestly told you that I have no degree in horticulture or botany; I'm just an ordinary person with long and practical experience raising house plants. Having tried and failed and finally succeeded with virtually every plant that can be grown successfully indoors, I wanted to share it with everybody.

Well, if you changed that around just a bit you'd have the philosophy of this book:

I am not a graduate of Escoffier or Cordon Bleu—I didn't even finish my correspondence course at the Bugs Bunny School of Carrot Cookery. I'm simply an ordinary person with practical experience in eating and cooking vegetable dishes. Having tried and failed and finally succeeded with lots and lots of vegetable recipes, I wanted to share the most Hassle-Free of them with you.

It wasn't easy weeding out the most Hassle-Free recipes. But it had to be done, so after wading through the hundreds of recipes handed down to me by friends, magazines, other cookbooks, and even occasionally my own slightly twisted mind, I have made my selections and am prepared to live with them.

Like Mother Earth's Guaranteed-to-Grow Plants, these are Mother Earth's Guaranteed-to-Taste-Good recipes. (I confess—even though I'm an expert gardener, there are some plants, like ferns, for instance, that simply will not do right for me. Same way with

FOREWORD

Give vegetable cookery a try.

recipes—many times I've come across dishes that sounded great on paper but tasted like paper when I finished whipping them up. Maybe it was me or maybe the recipe, but in either event none of those have been included in these pages.)

You *will* find, however, all sorts of delectables from Soup to Nuts, utilizing almost every vegetable from A to Z. Notice I said almost. I don't intend to burden you with recipes that require rare and exotic legumes; there'll be no Truffle Torte, for instance. But you'd be surprised—almost any vegetable you really need can be found almost any time of the year in your local supermarket. If not fresh, which is of course always preferable, you'll surely be able to find every ingredient in the Hassle-Free recipes either canned or frozen.

In the following pages we'll get into how to select the best produce and, here and there, sprinkled throughout, will be tips on growing your own—vegetables and herbs, that is.

But most importantly, I want to get you into the kitchen to give these recipes—and vegetable cookery—a try.

Please.

I promise you'll discover your food bill will come way down, your meals will be adventures into new tastes and textures, and you'll probably find that cooking and inventing your own recipes will take your mind off lots of your everyday problems. Just as much as does feeding and watering your plants.

There's no doubt you may be a bit nervous about serving a "Vegetables Only" meal to special dinner guests—whether they be family, friends, or business V.I.P.s. Well, don't be, because good food is good food whether it's Veal Parmesan or Eggplant Parmesan—in fact, the Eggplant Parmesan will probably get you a standing ovation. There is no need for the slightest temerity about cooking an all-vegetable meal for anybody—but, if in the end, you really panic and just *have* to add some shrimp to the sukiyaki, go right ahead. I know the feeling.

Finally, please remember that all of these recipes have been kitchen tested by Mr. Mother Earth himself—and if I can make 'em, anybody can!

Especially you.

Why Vegetables?

If you are what you eat, then I'm an eggplant in man's clothing.

But I am not alone. Be it for health, philosophical ideas, or just plain budget woes, more and more people are turning to meatless diets here in the eighties.

Some would like to eliminate animal flesh from their food plan, but because we are a meat-oriented society, most people believe that when you boil it down, a carrot's just a carrot and a potato's just a spud.

WRONG!

Vegetables harbor an infinitely larger trove of taste treasures than does meat, with its basic Big Three of Beef, Lamb, and Pork, or chicken with its inevitable indistinguishability from rubber. Scrape the crust off any chicken—fried, broiled, barbecued, store-bought, home-made, you name it—and I dare you to tell me it has any distinguishing characteristics other than wet or dry!

Please note that I do not use the word "vegetarian" in describing either my diet or the recipes in this book. Vegetarianism, in its literal sense, is too restricting, at least for me. A strictly vegetarian diet is defined as one that rules out consumption of at least four of the five animal foods—red meat, poultry, seafood, eggs, and dairy products. Orthodox vegetarians won't even *wear* animal products, let alone eat them.

Orthodox vegetarians won't even wear animal products.

WHY VEGETABLES?

In my diet I eliminate neither eggs nor dairy products—cheeses, milk, sour cream, etc. In the first place, there are just too many goodies one can make with these foods, and even more importantly, they are all a good source of many necessary nutrients—especially protein—that are taken away with the pheasants and filets. (I even eat fish once in a while.)

I suppose there will always be people who will trot out "facts" that prove you must inevitably get rickets or shrink down to ninety-eight pounds if you eat a strictly vegetable diet. Well, don't tell that to Bill Walton, center for the San Diego professional basketball team, who, while eating a strictly vegetarian diet has managed to become seven foot three and muster up enough strength and energy to earn a million dollars a year! Plato, Socrates, George Bernard Shaw, Steve Martin, Cheryl Ladd, even Isaac Newton—all vegetarians.

Furthermore, elephants won't go near anything but vegetables and even the most ferocious meat-eater won't tangle with a Pachyderm. Man o' War or Secretariat never saw a steak or a lamb chop, but I defy any meat-eating animal to keep pace with them.

The Who's Who of vegetable eaters is a long one, but we're not here to drop names, just recipes.

I certainly don't mean to gloss over the importance of maintaining a proper vitamin and mineral balance. However, it is safe to say that a diet which includes lots of leafy green vegetables, lots of fruits and nuts, lots of low-fat cheese and other dairy products, and an occasional egg will give you virtually all the vitamins and minerals you will need for good health and high energy. The only exception might be iron. Unless you can eat lots and lots and lots of raisins and spinach, you'll probably need a supplement.

By the way—a great many of these recipes call for sugar. White sugar is a last resort—try to substitute brown sugar or honey or fructose whenever possible.

Another thing: Before making any radical change in your diet, I strongly urge you check with your family doctor or nutritionist to be sure the diet is safe for you and discover what vitamin supplements, if any, are necessary to maintain good health.

Finally, I wouldn't ask any of you who are eating meat or poultry to quit—please forgive me—cold turkey. Instead, just ease on in.

Jockeys may eat meat, but Secretariat never saw a steak.

Instead of meat every night, cut down to, say, five nights, then four, maybe three . . . see if you're not eating every bit as well, enjoying your meals more, having lots of fun cooking, and of course, saving tons of money besides.

Okay. Now that you're convinced that a vegetable/dairy regimen is both safe and delicious, where should we go next?

Read on. I'll think of something.

Menu Planning

Let us presume you are about to take your first step into vegetable cookery. Where to begin? What dishes to start with? What dishes go with what others? Decisions, decisions . . .

Please. Not to worry. It's as easy as pie, which incidentally is not so easy for me since baking is not my best thing. You won't find many pie recipes in this book.

First, I'm going to assume your main concern is what to cook for dinner, since breakfast and lunch pretty much take care of themselves.

Although there are mavericks who prefer fettucine verde and garlic bread for their morning meal, I am a victim of my environment, as you probably are, too. My breakfasts consist of things like eggs and cereal and pancakes and fruit. Sometimes, of course, I go a little farther out—big omelets with vegetables and cheese, Eggs Benedict (every bit as good without the ham), or perhaps a succulent dish of fruit or cheese blintzes. But breakfasts are fairly simple, and it's just a matter of mixing up the fare so the day's most important meal does not become the day's most boring one. In fact, there's no reason why *any* meal should be boring, including lunch, since lunch can be anything you might ordinarily eat for breakfast or dinner—eggs, salads, sandwiches, stews.

I know you're wondering what to put on the plate for your first all-vegetable meal. It's good to begin by realizing that in serving a meatless meal, you have the opportunity to try three or four "main dishes" instead of the usual meat, green vegetable, and potato.

For instance, a meal beginning with a fruit and avocado salad, followed by stuffed mushrooms, then a fluffy corn soufflé, and finally flan for dessert will provide lots of tastes and leave you and your friends or family as stuffed as the mushrooms. (Incidentally, the above menu is not the most Hassle-Free kind of dinner to prepare—soufflés

Decisions, decisions . . .

Use your leftovers creatively.

require perfect timing and should really be left until later in your cooking experience, but it does show how easy it is to mix-and-match in meatless cooking.)

Now, then. Which of the myriad meatless main dishes to choose? Obviously, it's easiest if you have a specific craving. Takes all the pressure off. Simply look under broccoli, squash, potatoes, or whatever your craving happens to be, pick a recipe that sounds good to you, then hie to the market and pick up the ingredients. When you go to the market, have four or five days cooking in mind so you won't have to run back three times a week. Most vegetables will stay fresh and crisp for at least four or five days in your refrigerator.

Be sure to use your leftovers creatively. Yesterday's steamed veggies, simmered in a bit of tomato sauce and olive oil, can become

Better a good, simple meal than a barely edible fancy one.

today's spaghetti sauce; potato peelings, dipped in batter and fried, are a taste treat you won't soon forget—and so on.

Actually, meatless meals have almost no rules. Omelets are as legitimate a main dish for dinner as they are for breakfast or lunch. In fact, last night I whipped up an omelet with mushrooms, onions, bell peppers, and cheese, spooned a heap of home-fried potatoes down next to it, and it was almost an hour before I could get up from the table!

A large, mixed vegetable salad with Roquefort dressing and a side of hot buttered pumpernickel bread is certainly more than enough to be an entire meal. How about a salad of butter lettuce and herb dressing, followed by the biggest baked potato you can find, stuffed with butter, cheddar cheese, sour cream, dill, and chopped olives? Properly presented surrounded by parsley, this is a main course you can serve to friends and listen to them mutter, "Now why didn't I think of that?'' And of course, sometimes just a salad, a rich, hearty soup, and some thick garlic bread can become a culinary delight.

Just try and give each meal a balance—if one dish is extra heavy, something covered in a sauce, make the rest of the meal fairly light; if something is tart, add a sweet; if your main dish is green, add something yellow or white for contrast. There's nothing quite as dull as a monochromatic meal. (And did you ever stop to realize—there's no such thing as blue food?)

Finally, in these early stages, you don't want to tackle anything that is going to take hours to cook—none of the recipes in this book should take more than an hour or two at most—and the big portion of *that* time in chilling or oven time.

Oh, by the way, speaking of oven time . . . always remember to set the timer. It's all too easy to forget what's cooking. The result: blackened cookware, ruined food . . . so get yourself a good loud cooking alarm.

In short, when it comes to menu planning, trust your judgment. If you're giving a dinner party, try for something with a bit of flair—but *only after you've successfully prepared it at least once.* Better to serve a good, simple meal than a barely edible fancy one. If you're alone, or you're only cooking for your family, keep it simple and don't be afraid to experiment a bit. Instead of just heating up some oil in your wok and stir-frying a heap of chopped-up veggies, add a little teriyaki sauce, or perhaps a tangy sweet-and-sour.

Don't be mesmerized by all the old "rules" of cooking and eating.

Make your own rules.

That way you can break them any time you feel like it.

Okay, gang! Let's go to the market!

Are organically grown vegetables worth the extra money?

At the Market

Before you head into the kitchen, you've got to go to the market—a fairly frightening experience these days when you can almost be sure of spending over ten dollars even in the express lane!

Notice I said the market, not your local health food store where most vegetables sold are organically grown. Not that I don't think the organically grown vegetables aren't better—without question, they are. But they're only worth the extra money if you can afford it. If you go to a large, competitive supermarket and shop carefully, you will find a full seasonal selection of fresh fruit and produce and will pay quite a bit less.

Before you leave for the market, make a list of *everything* you need. It's depressing and time-consuming to discover you've overlooked buying one or two key ingredients and have to shlep all the way back.

Probably the most important thing in marketing is choosing the freshest fruits and vegetables. How to tell you're getting the best greens for your green? Easy. First, look for firmness. Better a little underripe than overripe. Secondly, beware of brown spots, holes, or other disfigurements. These do not necessarily indicate inedible veg-

I can get fresh garlic for almost nothing.

gies, but take a little more time to pick produce that is as cosmetically pleasing as you can find. Stay away from things that are out of season—summer squash may be available in the winter, but the squash is oh-so-small and not near as juicy and tasty (or inexpensive) as it should be.

Here's a little reminder that I'm almost embarrassed to pass on because it ought to go without saying—but since I have actually slipped up a few times myself, I'm going to remind you to WASH

YOUR VEGETABLES THOROUGHLY BEFORE COOKING. I mean *thoroughly*! Get all the earth that might be stuck in the crevices of the artichoke leaves; get all the sand out of the spinach. Scrub down the skin of potatoes or any other vegetable you're going to eat cooked with the peel on (the healthiest and most nutritious way in almost every instance—and tasty, too!). Don't peel your mushrooms but rub them firmly under cold water, both top side and under side. Wash each lettuce leaf individually. And so on. You never know what in the world may have attached itself to produce even if it's been organically grown and even though 99.999 percent of any dirt that might be on your veggies will be perfectly harmless, for the tiny amount of time it takes, make sure that every vegetable is squeaky-clean.

With regard to herbs and spices: most herbs can be grown in your own kitchen or patio as long as you have good sunlight and follow the directions on the seed packets you can buy at any nursery.

Fresh herbs are also usually available at the supermarket.

I personally see no reason to spend money buying dried marjoram in a bottle when I can grow my own for one-tenth the price. It makes no sense to buy garlic powder when I can get fresh garlic for almost nothing and scare off vampires in the bargain.

But, if you want to make your cooking *totally* Hassle-Free in the beginning, buy the spices off the rack. This would be a no-no if we were talking true, gourmet cooking—but for okay cuisine, go on and use the dried, store-bought herbs and spices. Sooner or later you'll come around.

The average American partakes of ten times more salt than is necessary.

Herbs and Spices

Two things are absolutely necessary to cook really delicious food: the first is heat of some kind, the second is spice of all kinds.

I have discussed the pros and cons of fresh herbs and spices vs. dried. (Fresh won, but dried *did* finish second.) It will only take a moment to run down most of the herbs and spices you see listed in most basic cookbooks, give you some general hints as to which spices and herbs go best with what foods, and any other little spicy tidbits I can come up with.

For instance: Think of herbs and spices as replacements for salt. It's pretty well accepted that too much salt will be harmful to your health, and it's also statistically true that each day the average American partakes of ten times more salt than is necessary! The remedy? Judicious use of herbs and spices and the removal of the salt shaker from the table.

You might want to know the difference between herbs and spices: A spice is any of various aromatic vegetable products such as nutmeg, curry, cloves, etc. used to season foods. An herb is a seed plant which does not develop woody persistent tissue, but is more or less soft and succulent, used for its scent and flavor.

HERBS AND SPICES

Here are the most important herbs and spices which, in a gesture toward organization, I have listed alphabetically.

ALLSPICE. If you believe this story, you also believe in the Easter bunny, but it sounded so good when I read it I'll pass it along: Seems that your basic seventeenth-century pirate, plundering and pillaging gaily along the Spanish Main, invented a method for preserving food, consisting of spicing and smoking, which was called *boucan* in French, thus causing pirates to become known as *Boucaniers* and finally Buccaneers.

The real point of the story is that the spice they used was Allspice. Which I suggest you use, too. But not for preserving food, merely to enhance flavor.

Add a bit of Allspice, ground or whole, to your favorite desserts and fruit dishes and you'll be pleasantly surprised.

Whether or not you want to wear an eye patch is unimportant.

ANISE. Still thought of as an aphrodisiac and a medicine for virtually every ailment from headache to epilepsy, Anise is the licorice-flavored base of many fruit and baked dishes and the after-dinner liqueurs such as Anisette and Pernod.

You'll enjoy the delicate taste of this herb in cookies and cakes—and if you ever feel really frisky, perhaps you might sprinkle some in a cup of tea before bedtime . . . .

BASIL. Basil was first discovered in Persia, where it became so deeply connected with religious rites that a Basil leaf in the grave was the occupant's passport to Heaven! Properly used in cooking, either fresh or dried, it can be your passport to culinary Heaven. You can use Basil in practically any dish at all, although the consensus of the most discerning palates, including mine, is that Basil goes best with tomatoes.

BAY LEAF. Also known as Laurel (and every bit as Hardy if you want to grow it yourself). It would take pages to fill you in on all the Laurel Lore available, beginning with stories from Greek Mythology all

Bay Leaf (Laurel) can add a distinctive touch to pasta.

the way through its use as headgear in Caesar's times (but not in Caesar salads) up through its extraordinary medicinal powers. Since this is a cookbook, however, and not a home course in herbal medicine, suffice it to say that the Bay Leaf, used discriminately, can add a very distinctive touch to mixed vegetables or even pasta dishes, and should bring you extra Laurels as a chef.

CARAWAY. According to the experts, Caraway is one of the oldest spices known, having been traced all the way back to the Stone Age. (Having never seen a fossilized Caraway Seed, I can't swear to the above.) As is true with all herbs and spices, the stories of its uses against demons and other lesser ills are legion—in fact, what better time to recommend a book called *Caravan to Casserole* by Malvina W.

Liebman, a small but potent work which will tell you fascinating stories about herbs and spices that you can digest at your leisure. For now, note only that Caraway Seeds are mainly used in breads, pastries, and any vegetables you wish to enhance. Use a light hand, as Caraway Seeds are pungent.

CHERVIL. Not exactly the "Smith" or "Jones" of Herbdom, Chervil can be used, fresh, as a substitute for Parsley, but basically it is an essential ingredient in the combination known as "Fines Herbes" used in many dishes but which I use most often in omelets. (The other ingredients in Fines Herbes: Parsley, Tarragon, and Chives.) I doubt you'll find Chervil fresh in your market, but if you do, don't slap it's face—chop it up and use it in your salad dressings, soups, and sauces.

CINNAMON. Cinnamon, either as bark or powdered, is so common and so good let me merely say you can use it in almost anything. It does not have to be restricted to use in desserts or hot chocolate. Put Cinnamon in anything you want. You may prefer the taste of Cinnamon on French Toast; your mate may love it with cottage cheese; your neighbor may crave it with baked apples. Personally, I most adore the taste of Cinnamon in lip gloss. And with that, we kiss the segment on Cinnamon good-bye.

CUMIN. Every now and again you'll run across a recipe callin' for Cumin. It will most probably be in a recipe for curry powder or a spicy Mexican dish, but it could just as well cum-in to use with beans, cheese, or bread. In which case it's called "Cumin Through the Rye."

CURRY POWDER. Perhaps my favorite taste. And also one which you're better off buying in dried form, because even if you were to take the time to grind and mix the twenty different herbs and spices that make up curry, it would still come out the same. Name the twenty spices? Oh, my weary bones . . . but you've been so very, very patient with me ("Cumin Through the Rye"?) I'll name you fifteen. They are: Allspice, Anise, Bay Leaves, Coriander, Cumin, Cardamom, Cloves, Cayenne Pepper, Fennel, Fenugreek, Ginger, Mace, Mustard, Black Pepper, and Turmeric. Whew! Now you see why it's better bought

Even if you were to mix the 20 spices, it would come out the same as curry you bought.

made up already? Anyway, try adding a bit of Curry Powder—sparingly at first and then increasing the amount to your taste—to things like eggs, salad dressings, and mixed vegetables. I think it will Curry your favor.

DILL. If you want to get your cucumbers into a pickle, Dill's the herb to call! You will also find that Dill sprinkled on salads, omelets, vegetables, or whatever will turn an average flavor into a real Dilly!

FENNEL. I'm so glad you've decided to give me one more chance. I will behave myself now and give you a straightforward, serious, and accurate description of Fennel. Fennel is a native of the Mediterranean area, where it needs lots of sun and not a great deal of water. It can also be successfully grown in kitchen windows. With a taste slightly resembling Anise, Fennel goes very well with salads, soups, breads, and vegetables. You will even enjoy the Fennel bulb, raw or boiled. Thank you for your attention.

GINGER. What's the first thing *you* think of when you think of Ginger? Gingerbread? Gingersnaps? Ginger on your Egg Nog? Ginger in your sweet sauces? We all think of different things when we think of Ginger. I think of Fred.

What's the first thing you think of when you think of Ginger?

MARJORAM. A truly blue-blooded (or would that be green-blooded) herb, having been said to have sprung from a dead King's breast. On the other side of the coin, Marjoram was also once commonly used in place of sawdust for sprinkling onto floors. It is now commonly used to enhance the taste of soups, cooked vegetables, and especially salads, confirmed by Shakespeare in *All's Well That Ends Well:* "Indeed, sir, she was the sweet marjoram of the salad, or rather the herb of grace." 'Nuff said. Who am I to try to top William Shakespeare?

MINT. For pure folklore, legend, and mythology no herb provides more exotica than Mint. There is a veritable mint of fascinating fables. Like the one about Pluto's wife Persephone getting so uptight when she found old Pluty-Baby was messing around that she stomped the lady to death, whereupon said dead lady turned into a Mint Plant. Mint has the usual quotient of ills it can cure, and is also thought to be an aid to virility. As an additive to food, a sprig or two of Mint is delicious sprinkled onto just about any salad or vegetable dish, and of course can be made into a delicious jelly. When you buy fresh Mint, and you simply must buy *only* fresh, make sure it's dark green, fully ripe, and strongly pungent. In short, be sure it's in Mint condition.

MUSTARD. Just about everybody thinks of Meat and Mustard in about the same way they think of Love and Marriage. Certain things just seem to go together, exclusive of any outside interference. Not that I think there's anything wrong with Meat and Mustard, it's just that it doesn't seem like "Hot Dog Americain" is a recipe that belongs in this cookbook. One of the best-kept secrets of the kitchen is that Mustard is great in and on lots of things! In its liquid form, especially Dijon Mustard, it's a must on cheese and avocado sandwiches, the basic ingredient in a delicious mustard and honey salad dressing, and a real treat in stuffed hard-boiled eggs; in its powdered form, Mustard spices up all manners of sauces and other good stuff.

NUTMEG. I hate to break the rhythm of this chapter but there's really nothing much to say about Nutmeg other than it tastes neat on desserts and even on a few vegetables like spinach and cauliflower. I

Mustard is great on lots of things besides meat.

tried very hard to be clever about this nifty herb, but it's merely further proof that nothing or no one is perfect. Except maybe Nutmeg.

OREGANO. (See MARJORAM) Honest.

PARSLEY. The universal garnish. If you've just eaten onions or garlic, a few pieces of Parsley will take your breath away. Next time you see Parsley on your plate, instead of putting it on the butter dish, eat it. You'll be pleasantly surprised.

POPPY SEEDS. If you think you can run outside and pick some Poppy Seeds and turn them into opium, think again. Then do what you want about it. A lower risk proposition, however, would be to sprinkle the Poppy Seeds on breads and rolls or perhaps on pasta or a vegetable stew. And that's no poppycock.

ROSEMARY. Rosemary has as romantic a history as her name. I mean, a sprig of Rosemary is often included in wedding bouquets! As for its culinary qualities, Rosemary's light, aromatic flavor can turn your ordinary succotash into something out of this world—Succotash with Rosemary. (About as Hassle-Free a recipe as you could think of.) Experiment a bit with Rosemary. Worse comes to worse, you can toss it to a bridesmaid.

SAFFRON. The Gucci, Tiffany, Cartier, etc. of spices. Saffron is so expensive that each "stigma" (a dried portion of the bud) is branded

Parsley will take your breath away.

with little S's. The reason the price is so high is quite simple: Each crocus blossom from which Saffron is derived has three stigmas, and each must be hand picked. It takes a hundred thousand stigmas to make a pound of Saffron, so by now I'm sure you've gotten the picture. Is Saffron worth the price? Will breads and cakes taste as good without it as with? Will Sylvia run off with Henry? Tune in tomorrow for the answers and other mind-boggling questions. Personally, I think Saffron is worth the price. I've never been accused of being prudent when it comes to food.

SAGE. Sage means wise, so be wise and always have Sage somewhere in your kitchen. You'll find it almost indispensable for cheese dishes and breads.

SESAME. Sesame was once a sacred spice, often used in funeral rituals to seek forgiveness for sin. You and I probably do not use it quite so esoterically. I sprinkle the seeds on bread or vegetable casseroles and occasionally use Sesame oil in salad dressings. It's too expensive an oil to use extensively. That's about it, folks. See you on *Sesame Street.* Just remember to holler "Open Sesame" to get in.

TARRAGON. A fairly new member of the herb and spice family, Tarragon was first uncovered in the late 1400s and was subsequently brought to us by the Colonists. It's not your all-purpose herb, but is vital to Bearnaise sauce, makes a nice addition to vinegar, and marries well with eggs. Maybe, as it grows older and begins to get the hang of things, it'll climb into the top ten spices. Meantime, Tarragon is just going to have to keep on learning through trial and error—yours!

THYME. Thyme is thought by many French chefs to be absolutely essential to any cuisine, but only in tiny, tiny amounts because it's a very pungent herb. When I use it—either dried leaves or fresh—I try to sprinkle it quickly and briskly into salads, soups, pasta sauces, or whatever, rubbing it between my palms. That way just enough gets into the food and I'm left singing "Thyme on My Hands."

The Kitchen

As they used to say in radio, "Ah-ah, don't touch that dial!" On your stove, that is.

You aren't ready to begin your adventure into cookery until your kitchen is properly equipped.

We'd all like one of those magnificent kitchens pictured in the "better" home magazines—you know, the ones with the stove as an island in the middle of the antique brick kitchen whose walls are virtually covered with copper pots and pans and every cooking tool on this planet and probably a couple from Saturn and Mars.

Alas, most of us can't afford this dream kitchen—but luckily, none of us really *needs* it.

There isn't a whole lot you can't cook and cook well if you have the following items:

— Saucepans (perhaps three or four of various sizes, preferably copper, but stainless steel will do and is considerably less expensive)

— Three frying pans or skillets, Teflon-coated, ranging from twelve inches in diameter down to six (an omelet pan is also a good idea, but not a necessity)

I love to browse in kitchenware places.

— Casserole dishes ranging from one quart to four quarts
— Three or four baking pans of different sizes and shapes (loaf, square, rectangular)
— Mixing bowls in various sizes
— Wooden stirring spoons
— Colander
— Rubber spatula
— Sharp knives (serrated, paring, slicing)
— Cleaver for chopping vegetables (indispensable in Chinese cooking where it's used for everything)
— Wok (makes stir-frying much easier, and can be used for almost anything you do in a skillet)
— Whisk (for beating egg whites, cream, and sauces)
— Brush for scrubbing vegetables
— Vegetable peeler
— Tongs
— Metal spatulas
— Measuring spoons
— Slotted spoon
— Long-handled fork
— Blender (an expensive food processor is fun to have, but for Hassle-Free cooking, a blender will do just fine)
— Vegetable steamer, to make vegetables that taste better (you can improvise a steamer with a metal colander and a saucepan, but there are many inexpensive ones available)

Of course you can add anything else that strikes your fancy in the kitchen supply shop. I love to browse in those kitchenware places. While I fantasize about owning that beautiful brass and copper espresso machine for several hundred dollars, I buy a very useful little garlic press for under two bucks (even though I know I can chop it up with a knife). As I marvel at the endless array of crocks, microwave ovens, cake molds, and the like, I find time to pick up a new measuring cup or an extra perforated metal spoon.

It's just like beginning the plant experience. Instead of going to the nursery and having the owner help you load up on the basics—pots, soil, fertilizer, hardy plants—go to a department store or a spe-

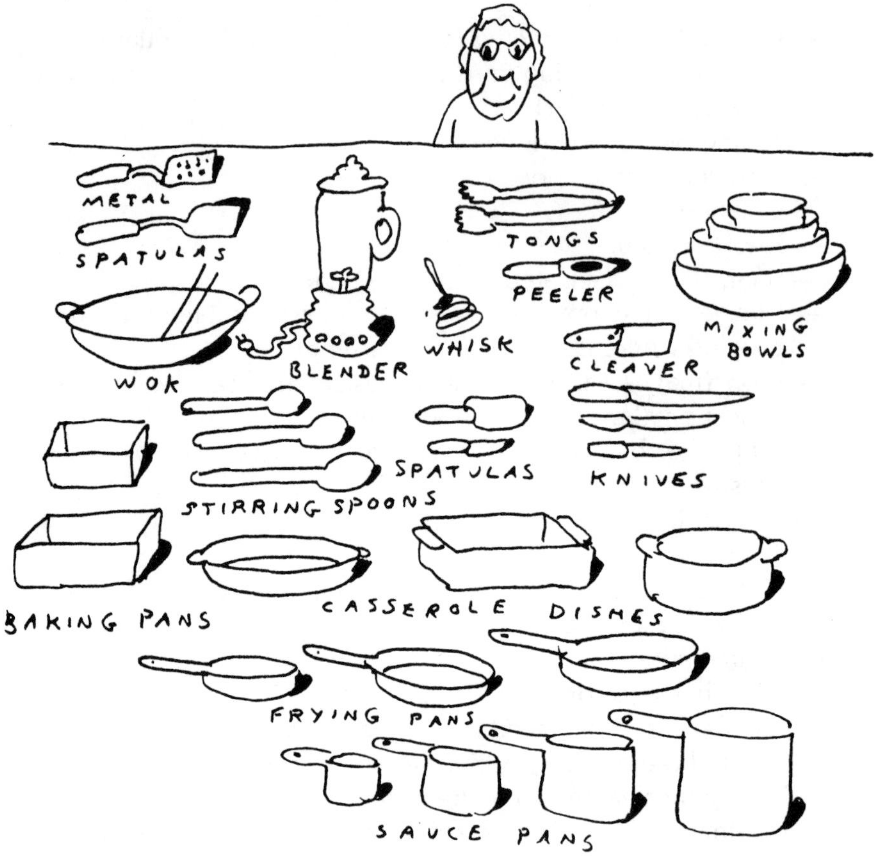

Basic kitchen needs.

cialty shop and ask them what you need for a complete, but not elaborate culinary set-up.

Okay. Seems like we've got just about everything we need to start down the Green-Brick road that's strewn with Artichokes and Zucchini and lots of other wonderments in between.

The time is now.

So let's get cooking!

From A to Z

At last, what you've been waiting for. The stars of our show—The Vegetables!!!

Since every Vegetable wanted first billing—and almost every one had a convincing argument—I have decided merely to list them in alphabetical order from A to Z.

I have included the vegetables which are most readily available fresh year around and the vegetables I prefer most myself. (I have left out Parsnips and Turnips, for instance, because neither one really turns me on.) And—in a fit of intelligence tantamount to learning how to breathe—I have listed my favorite recipes for each vegetable immediately following the description and incidental trivia on each.

So onward. First read—then eat—your way from Artichokes to Zucchini.

I'm sure you won't get fed up.

ARTICHOKES

Permit me to introduce the vegetable with a heart—the artichoke. Actually, artichokes are members of the Thistle family. And they were first discovered in Thistley! I mean, *Sicily*! They grow tall and feathery-looking, and that big bud on top, which will open into a breathtaking purple and blue flower if not cut off, is the artichoke, veritably screaming at passersby to "Eat my heart out!" (Forgive the continual reference to the artichoke's heart, but prepared in *any* way—boiled, marinated, hot, cold—artichoke hearts are very close to *my* heart when it comes to taste treats in veggie-land.)

Artichokes are generally available all year round, but are almost half the price during the spring and summer that they are during the

Before eating artichokes cut off the top third.

fall and winter. If you plan on growing your own artichokes, you can expect practically an all-year crop in the more temperate climates and a good spring-through-fall yield in colder spots.

Most people simply eat their artichokes boiled, and there's certainly nothing wrong with that. The tender tips, dipped in melted butter with a touch of garlic or even mayonnaise or any number of dips or even plain, are really delicious, but there are other, even more rewarding ways to cook artichokes, as you will see in a moment.

Before cooking an artichoke, cut off the top one-third, since you won't eat that anyway, and each leaf's got a tiny but ouchy little thorn on the end. And if you're going to stuff an artichoke, those spiny little suckers can really smart!

ARTICHOKES

To boil:

Wash artichokes. Cutt off stem at base and remove small outer leaves. With kitchen shears or sharp knife, clip any remaining thorny tips from leaves.

Stand artichokes upright in large deep saucepan. Use an enamel or stainless steel pain for cooking. Cast iron or aluminum utensils or carbon steel knives should not be used as they will discolor artichokes and give them a metallic taste.

Add water to cover and 2 tablespoons lemon juice. Cover and boil gently 35 to 45 minutes or until base can be pierced easily with fork.

Remove with slotted spoon and drain upside down. Artichokes can be served hot or cold, with butter, mayonnaise, or dips.

Artichokes may be cooked ahead. They will keep several days, covered, in the refrigerator. Reheat by returning them to simmering water 5 to 10 minutes or until heated through.

To stuff:

If artichokes are to be stuffed, firmly press each artichoke, crown down, on cutting board to spread leaves. With spoon, scoop out choke from center, then gently spread leaves and add stuffing.

Two dips for artichokes:

CREAMY DIP

½ cup sour cream
½ cup mayonnaise
1½ tablespoons chopped chives
1 tablespoon horseradish
½ teaspoon salt

In a bowl combine sour cream, mayonnaise, chives, horseradish, and salt. Chill. Garnish with additional chives.

Makes 1 cup.

FANCY BUTTER SAUCE

1 cup butter or margarine
¼ cup lemon juice
¼ cup freshly chopped parsley
1 teaspoon salt
½ teaspoon dry mustard
Dash hot pepper sauce

Melt butter in small saucepan. Add lemon juice, parsley, salt, mustard, and hot pepper sauce. Cook over low heat 5 minutes. Stir before serving.

Makes about 1¼ cups.

ARTICHOKE CHEESE SQUARES

2 tablespoons oil
⅓ cup finely chopped onion
1 clove garlic, mashed
4 eggs
1 14-oz. can artichoke hearts, drained
¼ cup dry bread crumbs
½ lb. Swiss cheese or sharp Cheddar cheese, shredded
2 tablespoons minced parsley
½ teaspoon salt; pepper to taste
¼ teaspoon oregano
⅛ teaspoon Tabasco sauce

Grease a 7 × 11-inch baking dish. Preheat oven to 325°.

In skillet, heat oil and sauté onion and garlic until limp but not brown.

Beat eggs to a froth in a mixing bowl, chop artichokes in small pieces and add to bowl. Stir in onion, crumbs, cheese, parsley, and seasonings.

Turn mixture into baking pan and bake for 25 to 30 minutes until set when lightly touched. Cut into squares.

Serves 6 to 8.

MARINATED ARTICHOKES

6 medium artichokes, cooked

Marinade:
1 cup oil
½ cup wine vinegar
2 tablespoons catsup
1½ teaspoons salt
1½ teaspoons oregano
1½ teaspoon minced garlic
¼ teaspoon pepper

In a jar with tight-fitting lid combine oil, vinegar, catsup, salt, oregano, garlic, and pepper. Cover and shake until blended.

Pour marinade evenly into artichokes. Cover and chill at least 12 hours. With slotted spoon, remove artichokes. Serve marinade as sauce for dipping leaves.

Serves 6.

ASPARAGUS

Asparagus is not my favorite vegetable. What am I going to do, sit here and ask you to believe that every single member of the edible vegetable kingdom is as good as the next? It's inevitable that as in all things subjective one man's meat—er, vegetable—will be another man's—oops, person's—poison, but I am also not going to sit here and tell you asparagus isn't good. Just plain boiled and buttered—well, frankly it wouldn't be my first pick on an à la carte menu. Add a Mornay or Hollandaise sauce, okay, not bad . . . but even the mammoth light-green spears served cold in a vinaigrette dressing don't exactly . . . wait a minute . . . what's happening? I swear I'm beginning to crave a dish of asparagus . . . .

Asparagus is not my favorite vegetable.

Whew! Forgive me. For a minute I was drifting off like a water lily in a quiet pond . . . a good way to get poetic and also squeeze in the little-known fact that asparagus is a genuine member of the Lily family. (Who cares?)

Asparagus will grow all year long practically anywhere, under the most difficult of conditions. You can even plant asparagus for ornamental purposes, as it grows into a tall, graceful feathery plant.

One last piece of Asparagus lore: In England, it's called Sparrow Grass.

Don't try to smoke it.

BOILED ASPARAGUS

Break or cut off the tough ends of the stalks and trim off the scales. Scrub the asparagus well with warm water and a soft brush to remove grit.

Place the asparagus in a deep, heavy skillet or shallow pan in 2 or 3 layers, thicker stalks on the bottom, thin on top. Cover with cold water till it stands ½-inch above the asparagus. Add ½ teaspoon each of salt and sugar or honey.

Keep pan uncovered. Bring to a full, rolling boil and let boil 1 to 4 minutes, depending upon the thickness of the asparagus and whether you prefer it crisp and chewy or a little softer.

Remove from heat and let stand uncovered at least 8 minutes or until ready to serve. The asparagus continues to cook while the water cools. If the wait is too long and the asparagus gets too cold, simply bring water to a boil again, drain, and serve immediately with butter or Hollandaise sauce.

Frozen asparagus takes less time with use of the same method. Start with solid-frozen asparagus, cover with cold water (½ inch over asparagus), bring to a full, rolling boil, separating stalks with a fork. Boil 1 minute, let stand, off heat, 4 minutes.

ASPARAGUS BENEDICT

2 tablespoons vegetable oil
1 clove garlic
4 eggs
Salt and pepper
1 bunch (2½ lb.) asparagus, cooked
½ cup grated Parmesan or Romano cheese
4 slices lightly buttered toast

Heat oil in skillet. Add garlic, cut in half, and cook slowly 1 minute. Push garlic to one side and drop eggs in oil, cover and cook slowly 3 minutes, or until eggs are done. Season with salt and pepper. Discard garlic.

Serve 1 egg and a little of the oil on each portion of hot asparagus. Sprinkle with cheese and serve on lightly buttered toast.

Serves 4.

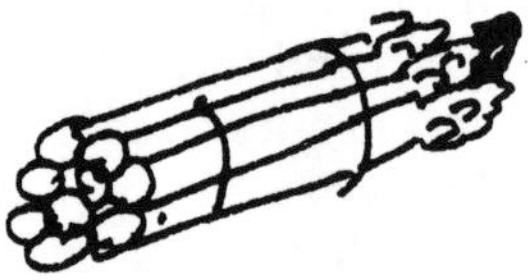

AVOCADO

Technically it's a fruit, but I'm going to include a couple of avocado ideas because the taste of a good, ripe avocado is in a class by itself.

They say that money doesn't grow on trees, but don't tell that to avocado growers! Since avocados are very seasonal, winter prices can be astoundingly high: I just came back from the market and the Guatamalan avocados—the thinner, lighter-green number—were 98¢ apiece . . . which come to think of it, by the time you read this might be cheap for the summer models!

Even though I promised myself that I wouldn't get into sandwiches in this book, I must confess that to rephrase an old cliché, "A sandwich without avocado is like a day without sunshine." What makes a better snack than avocado, Jack cheese, and bean sprouts with mayonnaise on dark bread or pita—or an avocado and tomato sandwich with a thin slice of Bermuda onion and some Dijon mustard . . . .

Remember—do not throw away that seed in the middle of the avocado! Planted directly into soil (don't waste time trying to root it in water), it will, about seven out of ten times, split at the top and send up a lovely plant that can grow into a forty-foot-tall tree if you happen to have a forty-foot tall living room.

Avocados are high in calories, so if you're dieting try to keep your intake light—but they're absolutely spilling over with iron and protein, so if you have no weight problems, always keep at least two avocados around: one ripe and ready, the other a couple of days away. (For quicker ripening, keep your hard, not-quite-ripe avocados in a dark place.)

Finally, mashed avocado, besides being the base for guacamole, is excellent just spread on a piece of bread. In fact, it used to be known as "Poor Man's Butter." But at today's prices, that must have been a long time ago.

If you're dieting—keep your avocado intake light.

AVOCADO-TOMATO SALAD

1 ripe avocado, peeled and diced
1 teaspoon lemon juice
2 medium tomatoes, peeled, seeded, and diced
2 tablespoons onions, minced
2 tablespoons finely chopped fresh parsley
1 teaspoon salt
Freshly ground black pepper
2 tablespoons red wine vinegar
¼ cup vegetable oil

Moisten the diced avocado with the lemon juice to prevent discoloration.

In a mixing bowl, combine the avocado, diced tomato, and minced onion. Add the parsley, salt, and a few grindings of pepper, and gently mix the ingredients togther.

With a fork or whisk, beat the vinegar and oil together, then pour it over the avocado and tomato mixture. Stir thoroughly and chill for at least an hour.

Serve as a first course on a bed of crisp lettuce.

Serves 6

AVOCADO-MUSHROOM SALAD

½ cup salad oil
3 tablespoons tarragon vinegar
2 tablespoons lemon juice
2 tablespoons water
1 tablespoon parsley, chopped
1 clove garlic, minced
¾ tablespoon salt
Dash pepper
2 avocados, peeled, pitted, and sliced
8 oz. fresh mushrooms, halved lengthwise (3 cups)
Parsley sprigs

In screw-top jar, combine oil, vinegar, lemon juice, water, chopped parsley, garlic, salt, and pepper. Cover and shake to blend.

Pour over avocados and mushrooms in a shallow dish. Chill several hours, spooning marinade over occasionally.

To serve, drain avocados and mushrooms; arrange on platter. Garnish with parsley sprigs.

Serves 8

GUACAMOLE DIP

2 large ripe avocados, diced
1 ripe tomato, peeled and diced
1 teaspoon salt
2 small hot peppers, finely diced
or
½ teaspoon Tabasco sauce
2 tablespoons lemon juice
⅛ teaspoon fresh-ground black pepper

Mash avocado, add tomato, onion, lemon juice, salt, pepper, and hot peppers or Tabasco. Mash until dip is smooth, or blend in blender. Let chill an hour or so before serving.

Serve with corn chips.

Makes 1¼ cups.

AVOCADO ICE CREAM

Don't say no until you've tried this lovely pale-green ice cream which has a very subtle tropical flavor.

1 fully ripe avocado
2 tablespoons lemon juice
2 tablespoons white corn syrup
½ teaspoon vanilla extract
½ teaspoon almond extract
1 quart vanilla ice cream, slightly softened

Peel the avocado, cut it in half, and remove seed. Mash firmly with a fork or spoon and then whirl in a blender for 30 seconds.

Add to avocado the lemon juice, white corn syrup, vanilla extract, and almond extract.

Combine mashed avocado mixture with ice cream, mixing well. Freeze until firm but not hard, at least 4 hours.

Serves 6

BEANS

Beans, beans, the musical fruit, the more we eat—

Beans come in an enormous variety of shapes and sizes: Lima Beans, Kidney Beans, Pinto Beans, Soybeans, String Beans, ad infinitum.

They all have one thing in common, however:

They are not only delicious, they are practically indispensable to good vegetable cookery. The Soybean, for instance, forms the base for many terribly convincing imitation meat (even sausage and bacon) dishes; you can even whip up a pretty good imitation turkey or chicken with a soy bean base. But these recipes are not Hassle-Free, and thus you won't find them here. (However, some of the packaged soy-meat products are simply delicious so don't be afraid to bring home some fake bacon once in a while.)

Beans grow on vines and are a fairly good year-round crop in temperate climates, although they take as long as three to four months to mature, depending on temperatures.

Baked beans, meatless chili, refried beans (frijoles)—the possibilities are endless. (See Bean Sprouts).

The soybean forms the base for many convincing imitation meat-flavored dishes.

Although we always must presume that fresh produce is best, beans can easily be obtained frozen or canned, and frankly, in this case, there isn't that great a difference.

Trust me. I am *not* full of beans!

BLACK BEANS AND RICE

1 16-oz. package dry black beans
6 cups water
2½ teaspoons salt
2 tablespoons salad oil
1 cup onion, chopped
1 cup green pepper, chopped
1 garlic clove, minced
1 8-oz. can tomato sauce
½ teaspoon pepper
4 cups hot cooked rice

Rinse beans in running cold water and discard shriveled beans. In 5-quart Dutch oven, over medium-high heat, heat beans, water, and salt to boiling. Boil 2 minutes. Remove from heat; cover and let stand 1 hour.

Do not drain beans. Over high heat, heat beans to boiling. Reduce heat to low; cover and simmer 40 minutes, stirring occasionally.

Meanwhile, in 10-inch skillet, over medium heat, in hot salad oil, cook onions, green pepper, and garlic until tender, stirring occasionally. Stir onion mixture, tomato sauce, and pepper into beans; cook an additional 20 to 40 minutes until beans are tender.

To serve, spoon beans over rice.

Serves 8

REFRIED KIDNEY BEANS

1½ cups dried red kidney beans
6 cups water
8 tablespoons vegetable oil
2 onions
2 tablespoons butter
1 clove garlic, minced (optional)
2 cups cooking liquid from beans
2 teaspoons salt
Grated cheese (Jack or mild Cheddar)

Rinse the beans and put them in a large pot with the water, 2 tablespoons vegetable oil, ½ onion, chopped, and 2 teaspoons salt. Bring the water to a boil, then turn down the heat, cover the pot, and simmer the beans gently for about 1½ hours. Remove the cover and cook the beans a little while longer, until they are completely tender and the remaining liquid is thick.

In a large heavy skillet, heat 6 tablespoons oil and the butter together. Chop the onions and sauté them in the oil and butter until they are golden. The garlic may be added at this point.

Add the beans and their 2 cups cooking liquid and lower the flame slightly. Cook the beans, stirring often, until most of the liquid has been absorbed. Mash some of the beans with a wooden spoon. Continue cooking and stirring for about ½ hour, until the beans have the consistency of a fairly thick paste.

Serve hot as a side dish, topped with grated cheese; or use as a filling for tacos.

Serves 4 to 6

SPANISH LIMA BEANS

1½ cups dry large lima beans
Water
1 teaspoon salt
¼ cup oil
1 small clove garlic, crushed
1 cup chopped onion
1 cup chopped green pepper or celery
1 tablespoon cornstarch
1 tablespoon chili powder
1 cup whole ripe olives (pitted)
¾ cup shredded American cheese

Soak beans overnight in about 1 quart water.

Cook beans until tender, about 1 hour. Add more water to cover if needed. Drain beans, reserving 1 cup bean liquid. Add salt. Set aside.

Heat oil in small skillet and sauté garlic, onion, and green pepper until tender.

In bowl combine cornstarch, chili powder, and 3 tablespoons cold water. Add beans, sauteed vegetables, bean liquid, olives, and half of cheese. Blend well. Pour into a 1½-quart casserole and sprinkle with remaining cheese.

Bake at 375° 20 minutes.

Serves 6

LENTIL BURGERS

2 cups cooked lentils
1 cup soft whole wheat bread crumbs
½ cup wheat germ
½ cup finely chopped onion
1½ teaspoons salt
2 eggs, lightly beaten
1 tablespoon Worcestershire sauce
3 tablespoons oil

Mash lentils slightly. Stir in bread crumbs, wheat germ, onion, salt, eggs, and Worcestershire sauce. Make patties, using ½ cup lentil mixture for each.

Heat oil in a large skillet. Cook patties until golden brown on both sides, about 5 minutes.

Serve on whole wheat pita bread, if desired

Makes 6 patties

BOSTON BAKED BEANS

4 cups dried peas or Great Northern beans
3 medium whole onions, peeled
2 teaspoons salt
4 cloves
½ cup molasses
1 cup brown sugar
2 teaspoons dry mustard
1 teaspoon black pepper
2 cups water

Put the beans in a large saucepan and pour in enough cold water to cover them by at least 2 inches. Bring to a boil, let boil 2 minutes, then let the beans soak in the water off the heat 1 hour. Bring to a boil again, add 1 onion, and 1 teaspoon salt. Half cover the pan and simmer the beans as slowly as possible about 30 minutes, or until they are partially done. Drain the beans and discard the onion and bean water.

Preheat the oven to 250°. To bake the beans, use a 2½-quart bean pot or a heavy casserole with a tight-fitting cover. Place 2 onions, each stuck with 2 cloves, in the bottom of the bean pot or casserole, and cover with the beans.

In a small mixing bowl, combine the molasses, ¾ cup of the brown sugar, mustard, and 1 teaspoon each of salt and pepper. Slowly stirring with a large spoon, pour in the 2 cups of water.

Pour this mixture over the beans. Cover tightly and bake in the center of the oven 4½ to 5 hours. Then remove the cover and sprinkle with the remaining ¼ cup brown sugar. Bake the beans uncovered another ½ hour and serve.

Serves 6

MEATLESS CHILI

2 cloves garlic, minced
1 large onion, minced
1 large celery stalk with leaves, chopped
1 small green pepper, diced
2 tablespoons oil, butter, or margarine
1 1-lb. can tomatoes
Salt and pepper
2 teaspoons chili powder
1 teaspoon cumin seeds
½ teaspoon thyme
½ teaspoon oregano
3 cups cooked soybeans
or
1 cup each cooked soybeans, pinto beans, and red kidney beans

Sauté garlic, onion, celery, and green pepper in oil until onion is tender.

Add tomatoes and liquid, break up, bring to a boil, and add salt and pepper to taste, chili powder, cumin seeds, thyme, and oregano. Simmer 10 minutes to blend flavors. Add beans and heat through.

If a more liquid chili is desired, add water or vegetable broth or bean liquid. Thicken with cornstarch or flour paste, if desired.

Serves 4 to 6

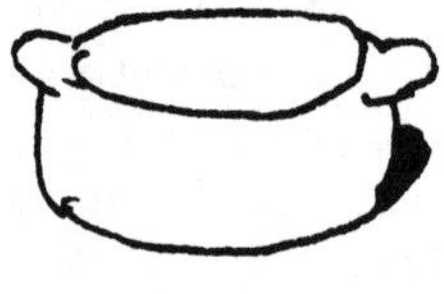

BEAN SPROUTS

Before moving on to our next vegetable (which for those of you who can't stand suspense will be Beets), let's spend just a moment and talk about a highly nutritious additive to salads, sandwiches, or just your empty stomach: Bean Sprouts. Besides having a subtle taste and amusing crunchiness, sprouts are rich in vitamins and minerals and are super for all of us dieters. Best of all, you can eliminate the middleman by purchasing the beans (or seeds) and sprouting them yourself.

The best place to hatch a sprout is in the kitchen, away from

Why buy sprouts?

too-bright light but in a spot where the temperature remains pretty much around 65 to 70°. The most common beans for sprouting—mung, soy, garbanzo, lima, kidney, navy, and pinto—may not all be available in your local market but are certainly easy to find at any natural or health food store. You can also sprout the seeds of alfalfa, mustard, sesame, barley, oats, and garden peas.

Begin by covering several dozen beans with water in a large, flat dish. Let them soak overnight, covered with plastic wrap to keep the air out. In the morning, empty out the water, line the dish with either cheesecloth or paper towels, keep the beans moist but not wet, and with any ordinary luck a majority of the beans will have sprouted to a harvestable length—a couple of inches—in about four days.

Sprouts are fun for the whole family, and since children can grow them by themselves, you're liable to see your kids not only eating but loving a food that's "good for them."

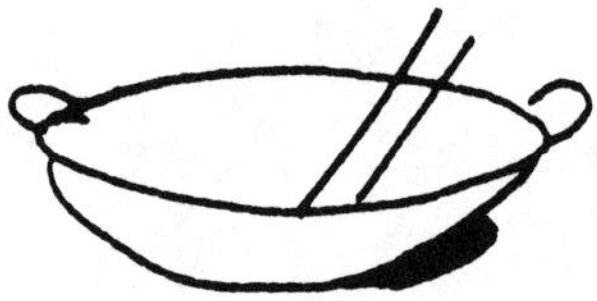

BEETS

I am a member of the "Beet Generation."

That's right, my friends. I am still sitting around coffeehouses plucking my guitar and singing the praises of beets, even though all of that went out of style twenty years ago.

You just can't beat a good beet. Beets are an underrated vegetable and have never gotten the publicity they deserve except on "American Bandstand" where kids used to say, "The words weren't so hot but I loved the beet."

Anyway, beets should be planted in very early spring so that in about two months you'll be ready to pluck. If you want to thin out your beet crop (which is recommended by both Mr. Mother Earth the plant man and Mr. Mother Earth the cook), the tiny "thinnings" and tops can be cooked.

Beets can be turned into Borscht, and the leaves can be steamed and substituted for spinach.

Beets can be sliced into thin strips, either cooked or raw, and used to complement almost any salad; they can be glazed with an orange sauce and served with Eggplant Piccata, or they can be turned into cold Borscht, a delicious opener, or, properly garnished, a meal in themselves. And of course the leaves can be steamed and substituted for spinach.

I could continue to sing the praises of this wonderful red vegetable, but I'd like to move on to the recipes for its use.

Besides, I've got to quit writing for a while.

I'm beat.

COLD BORSCHT

8 beets, washed and peeled
1 onion, chopped fine
2½ quarts water
1 tablespoon salt
⅓ cup lemon juice
3 tablespoons sugar
2 eggs
Sour cream for garnish

Combine the beets, onion, water, and salt in a saucepan. Bring to a boil and cook over medium heat for 1 hour. Add the lemon juice and sugar and cook for 30 minutes. The soup may require a little more sugar or lemon juice, depending upon the sweetness of the beets.

Beat the eggs in a bowl. Gradually add 3 cups of the soup, beating constantly to prevent curdling. Return this mixture to the balance of the soup, beating steadily. Remove all of the beets from the soup.

Grate 5 of the beets and return them to the soup. If a very thick soup is desired, place the remaining beets in the blender with 2 cups of the soup, and blend until the mixture is smooth. Add the mixture to the soup.

Chill the soup and serve very cold with a spoonful of sour cream in each dish.

Serves 8

BEETS WITH ORANGE SAUCE

6 cups water
1 teaspoon salt
2 tablespoons tarragon vinegar
1½ lb. small beets, washed but unpared
2 tablespoons butter or margarine
1 tablespoon cornstarch
⅓ cup sugar
1 cup orange juice
1 cup fresh orange segments, cut up

In a large saucepan bring water, salt, and vinegar to a boil. Add beets and cook over moderately low heat until tender. Cooking time will depend on the size of the beets, and can range from 30 minutes to 2 hours. Test tenderness with a fork; when beets are easily pierced with the fork, drain beets. Then plunge them into cold water.

Just as soon as they are cool enough to handle, trim off bottom root and any top stems. Slip off the skins. Cut beets into ½-inch crosswise slices.

In a large saucepan melt butter over moderately low heat; blend in cornstarch and sugar. Gradually stir in orange juice and continue to cook until thickened, stirring constantly.

Add sliced beets and orange segments to the orange sauce and cook over low heat until heated through.

Serves 6 to 8

BROCCOLI

According to expert sources, broccoli is the best all-around cole (cabbage and its close relatives) crop for the home gardener because it bears practically all year long and is very easy to grow.

According to me, broccoli is a very useful vegetable for the home cook because of its distinctive flavor and ability to function either cooked or raw in a large variety of dishes.

Because there is not a whole lot of lore available on broccoli, and because quips and puns on this delightful vegetable are hard to come by, let me merely suggest that when purchasing broccoli make sure it's a deep, rich green without any yellow and that it's firm in the stalk—wilting and discoloring are signs of old age in broccoli.

As they are in just about everything.

Wilting and discoloring are signs of old age in broccoli.

BROCCOLI CUSTARD

2 lb. broccoli, cut into 2-inch pieces
4 eggs, beaten
2 cups creamed cottage cheese
1 8-oz. can whole kernel corn
⅓ cup chopped green onion
1 cup shredded Cheddar cheese
Dash hot pepper sauce
Salt and pepper
¼ cup butter
Seasoned bread crumbs

Place broccoli in a greased 11 × 7 × 2-inch dish.

Combine eggs and cottage cheese in large bowl and mix well. Add drained corn, green onion, cheese, hot pepper sauce, and salt and pepper to taste. Pour over the broccoli.

Melt butter and combine with bread crumbs. Sprinkle over top of casserole. Bake at 350° for 45 minutes. Let sit a few minutes before serving.

Serves 6 to 8

STEAMED BROCCOLI

Wash broccoli and trim off tough stem ends. Cut broccoli into spears, slitting thick stems almost to heads.

Put broccoli in steamer and steam until tender, probably 8 to 10 minutes.

Serve with butter or cheese sauce—or top with melted butter and sprinkle with grated Parmesan cheese or slivered almonds.

BROCCOLI-RICE BAKE

This is a particularly good quick, Hassle-Free dish for two.

2½ tablespoons finely chopped onion
2 teaspoons butter or margarine
1 10-oz. package frozen chopped broccoli, cooked and drained
½ small clove garlic, crushed (optional)
1 cup cooked rice
2½ tablespoons grated Parmesan cheese
2 eggs, lightly beaten
¼ cup milk
½ teaspoon salt
Dash pepper
½ cup shredded Mozzarella cheese

Sauté onion in butter until tender, but not brown. Add broccoli, garlic, rice, Parmesan cheese. Mix well.

Combine eggs, milk, salt, and dash of pepper. Stir into rice mixture

Turn into a well-greased shallow 1-quart casserole. Top with cheese and bake at 350° for 20 to 25 minutes or until set.

Serves 2

BRUSSELS SPROUTS

I'll bet you thought I was going to start this off by saying "Brussels Sprouts" are little Belgians. Well, think again, because even *I* would not stoop that low.

Brussels sprouts, however, *are* little cabbages, at least they're a relative of cabbage.

Unlike cabbage, brussels sprouts are usually not eaten raw, but rather steamed or lightly boiled with a bit of butter or a light cheese sauce.

Frankly, brussels sprouts can stand alone because their flavor is rather strong. There are, however, a couple of recipes for sauces which are Hassle-Free and extremely tasty. I would be remiss not to pass them on.

BRUSSELS SPROUTS MOUSSE

2 lb. Brussels sprouts
1 pint whipping cream
4 envelopes unflavored gelatin
1½ cups water
1 teaspoon salt
⅛ teaspoon white pepper
2 teaspoons lemon juice
¼ teaspoon onion juice
1 cup sour cream
1 cup dry white wine
Dilled Sour Cream

Cover and cook brussels sprouts in 1 inch of boiling salted water for 10 to 15 minutes or until tender. Drain.

Blend in blender with whipping cream.

Sprinkle gelatin over water in saucepan. Soften 5 minutes, then dissolve over low heat. Add salt, pepper, lemon and onion juices. Blend with brussels sprouts puree, sour cream, and wine.

Pour into 2-quart mold. Chill until firm.

Unmold and serve with Dilled Sour Cream.

DILLED BRUSSELS SPROUTS

2 lb. fresh brussels sprouts
2 tablespoons butter or margarine
¼ cup water
1 teaspoon dill seed
Salt and pepper

Wash and drain brussels sprouts and remove any blemished leaves. Trim off stems.

Combine brussels sprouts, butter, water, dill, and salt and pepper to taste in saucepan. Cover and bring to a boil. Reduce heat and simmer 10 minutes or until brussels sprouts are fork tender. Serve at once.

Serves 8

DILLED SOUR CREAM

1 pint sour cream
2 tablespoons prepared horseradish
1 teaspoon dill weed
1 teaspoon salt

Blend sour cream, horseradish, dill weed, and salt.

Serves 6 to 8

CABBAGE

"The time has come, the Walrus said, to talk of many things; Of shoes and ships and sealing wax, of cabbages and kings."

I speak of cabbage.

In researching my "lore library" for information on cabbage and brussels sprouts I came up with some interesting trivia, the most interesting being that cabbage is the birthday plant for September 19. It was interesting to me because I never knew there were birthday plants for individual days of the month, but rather than research them all, I merely suggest you pick your favorite vegetable, call it your birthday plant, and serve yourself a huge helping on that day.

The cabbage family is easy to grow where summers are not too hot, long, or dry.

FROM A TO Z

There are many members of the cabbage family, including brussels sprouts and the king of cabbages, cauliflower. Cabbage is delicious either cold or hot; brussels sprouts are best when simply boiled, lightly seasoned and buttered; and cauliflower, of course, is wonderful cold, dipped in a cheese- or onion-flavored sauce or hot, au gratin.

All members of the cabbage family are fairly easy to grow where summers are not too hot, long, or dry.

I think you'll find some very good cabbage recipes below.

Including corned beef and cabbage.

Except I left out the corned beef.

SWEET AND SOUR STUFFED CABBAGE

This recipe takes a little more time then most of the ones in this book, but it's worth it.

1 large cabbage
1½ cup raisins
¾ cup boiled rice
2 tart apples, pared and chopped
2 onions, chopped
1½ cups brown sugar, packed
½ tablespoon salt
4 tablespoons butter or margarine
¼ teaspoon cinnamon
1 large can tomatoes (16 oz.)
1 8-oz. can tomato sauce
½ cup lemon juice

Cut out and discard core of cabbage. Place remainder in boiling water for approximately 20 minutes or until leaves are tender enough to peel away. Drain and cool cabbage. Cut out any thick ribs from stem ends.

In a skillet, cook onions in butter until clear but not browned.

Combine cooked rice, apples, onions, and butter, ½ cup sugar, salt, ½ cup raisins, and cinnamon. Place a ball of 2 heaping teaspoons of mixture in the center of each cabbage leaf, wrapping and smoothing the cabbage around the rice ball, overlapping all the edges as securely as you can.

In a large Dutch oven, combine the tomatoes (if whole, cut up) with tomato sauce, lemon juice, 1 cup sugar, raisins, and any leftover cabbage leaves chopped up. Place cabbage balls in the sauce. Cook over low heat for 2 hours.

This can be refrigerated or frozen and reheated in a 350° oven for 15 minutes before serving.

Serves 6 to 8

BROWNED CABBAGE AND NOODLES

3 lb. cabbage
1 tablespoon salt
1½ sticks (⅜ lb.) butter
3 tablespoons grated onion
2 teaspoons sugar
½ teaspoon freshly ground black pepper
1 lb. broad noodles, cooked and drained

Wash the cabbage and grate very fine. Mix in the salt and let stand 2 hours. Rinse, drain, and dry.

Melt half the butter in a deep large skillet or Dutch oven. Mix in the cabbage, onion, sugar, and pepper. Cook over low heat 1¼ hours, stirring frequently. Add the remaining butter after 1 hour. Toss in the cooked noodles until thoroughly mixed with the cabbage. Cook over low heat for 5 minutes.

Serves 6 to 8

CAROL'S SWEET COLESLAW DRESSING

1 cup mayonnaise
1 tablespoon honey
1 tablespoon mustard

Mix well. Toss into coleslaw.

SWEET AND SOUR RED CABBAGE

3 tablespoons butter
½ cup chopped onion
8 cups shredded red cabbage
1 apple, peeled and diced
1 cup water
3 tablespoons cider vinegar
2 tablespoons sugar
1½ teaspoons salt
¼ teaspoon pepper
¼ cup raisins (optional)

Melt the butter in a saucepan; sauté the onion for 5 minutes. Mix in the cabbage; cover and cook over low heat for 5 minutes.

Add the apple, water, vinegar, sugar, salt, and pepper. Cover and cook over low heat for 30 minutes, stirring frequently. Add the raisins, if desired; cook for 5 minutes longer.

Serves 4 to 6

CAROL'S COLESLAW

1 head cabbage
1 carrot
¼ head red cabbage

Wash cabbage and remove any wilted leaves. Wash and peel carrot.

Grate cabbage and carrot and mix together. Toss with a sweet or a sour dressing before serving. If you like marinated coleslaw, toss with dressing and refrigerate for a few hours.

POPPY SEED COLESLAW DRESSING

½ cup honey
½ cup vinegar
2 tablespoons oil
1 tablespoon poppy seeds
1 teaspoon salt
1 teaspoon dry mustard
¼ teaspoon onion powder

Blend honey, vinegar, oil, poppy seeds, salt, mustard, and onion powder in blender. Toss into coleslaw.

Serves 6

CARROTS

As a child you were no doubt admonished to eat lots of carrots because they're excellent for your eyesight. I think that's probably true, because I've never seen a carrot wearing glasses. It's also probably true because carrots are very rich in vitamin A.

When it comes to carrots, think small.

Carrots come in two parts—tops and bottoms. Carrot tops are a great addition to any kind of "green" drink or soup.

The bottoms are wonderful either raw or cooked. The most important thing to remember when selecting carrots is that bigger is *not* better. In fact, carrots are at their most delicious and tender when only about half-grown, so don't think you'll be getting more for your money by purchasing the longest, fattest carrots in the market. When it comes to carrots, think small.

Fresh carrot juice is delicious and overflowing with health-giving qualities, but carrots are tough to squeeze unless you have an expensive juicer, so you'll have to buy your carrot juice, usually found only at health stores.

There are lots of things you can do yourself with carrots, however, other than just steaming or boiling and serving them with butter. So here are some recipes, which you should be able to read without any problems if you remember to eat lots of carrots.

ORANGE CARROTS

8 carrots
⅓ cup butter or margaine
½ cup brown sugar, packed
½ cup orange juice
1 tablespoon grated orange peel
2 tablespoons honey
¼ teaspoon cinnamon

Peel carrots and cook in boiling water until barely tender. Drain.

Melt butter and brown sugar in saucepan and stir in orange juice, orange peel, honey, and cinnamon. Add carrots and simmer uncovered for 5 to 7 minutes, until liquid is thick.

Serves 6 to 8

BRANDIED CARROTS

1 lb. carrots
3 tablespoons water
4 tablespoons butter or margarine
½ teaspoon salt
2 tablespoons brandy
Toasted slivered almonds

Peel carrots and cut in very thin diagonal slices. Place in saucepan with water and 3 tablespoons butter, salt, and brandy. Cover tightly and cook over moderate heat until liquid is absorbed and carrots are barely tender.

Add remaining 1 tablespoon butter and a generous sprinkle of almonds. Mix well.

Serves 4 to 6

CARROT LOAF

3 cups cooked carrots
4 eggs
1 teaspoon salt
3 tablespoons sugar
1 tablespoon cornstarch
1½ tablespoons water
1 pint light cream
¼ teaspoon nutmeg
3 tablespoons oil or melted butter
Dash ginger

Puree cooked carrots in blender. Beat eggs till frothy and add to carrots in blender.

Blend with sugar, salt, and butter. Combine cornstarch and water, stirring well to dissolve lumps. Add to puree. Pour in cream and nutmeg. Blend well.

Pour into greased baking dish and place in pan of hot water. Bake at 350° for about 45 minutes. Serve hot.

Serves 6

CARROT CAKE

- **2 cups sifted flour**
- **2 teaspoons baking powder**
- **1½ teaspoons soda**
- **1 teaspoon salt**
- **2½ teaspoons cinnamon**
- **2 cups sugar**
- **1½ cups oil**
- **4 large eggs**
- **2¾ cups coarsely grated carrots**
- **1 8½-oz. can crushed pineapple, drained**
- **¾ cup chopped walnuts or pecans**
- **1 cup shredded coconut**
- **Cream Cheese Frosting**

Sift together flour, baking powder, soda, salt, and cinnamon. In a large bowl, mix sugar, oil, and eggs.

Add flour mixture a little at a time, mixing well after each addition. Add carrots, pineapple, nuts, and coconut and blend thoroughly. Turn into 3 greased and floured 9-inch round baking pans. Bake at 350° for 45 minutes.

Cool about 10 minutes before removing from pans. Cool completely and frost between layers and top with Cream Cheese Frosting. Carrot Cake will keep well in the refrigerator up to 1 week.

CREAM CHEESE FROSTING

- **½ cup butter or margarine**
- **1 8-oz. package cream cheese**
- **1 teaspoon vanilla**
- **1 1-lb. package confectioner's sugar**

Soften butter and cream cheese. Cream together with vanilla. Sift in confectioner's sugar and blend well. If too thick, add 1 teaspoon milk to thin to spreading consistency.

CARROT BREAD

2 eggs
1 cup sugar
⅔ cup oil
1½ cups flour
¾ teaspoon soda
1 teaspoon cinnamon
1 teaspoon nutmeg
½ teaspoon salt
1½ cups finely grated carrots
1 cup chopped walnuts
¾ cup raisins

Beat eggs with sugar and oil.

Sift together flour, soda, cinnamon, nutmeg, and salt. Add to egg mixture. Beat well. Add carrots, nuts, and raisins.

Grease large loaf pan, and pour in mixture. Bake at 350° for 1 hour.

CAULIFLOWER

Cauliflower was discovered in 1933 when Jack Dempsey looked at his ears and . . . Forgive me. I must be getting punchy.

Cauliflower is actually a member of the cabbage family—in fact, Mark Twain called it "merely a cabbage with a college education." (I suppose that's because it looks like a large, white brain.)

Cauliflower can be grown indoors or out, especially where the climate is cool and humid. Because it doesn't do well during the dry summer months, that's when you'll find it's most expensive.

You may have to get used to the rather strong taste of cauliflower, but if you do, it can be eaten raw with your favorite dip or cooked, either boiled or steamed. A bit of butter or cheese sauce will enhance it immeasurably.

Mark Twain contemplating a head of cauliflower.

FROM A TO Z

There's an unusual type of cauliflower called "Purple Head" which instead of the usual white color is—well, I'll leave you to try and work out the answer. The thing is, this variety of cauliflower turns *green* when cooked. You may want to try it since it's got a slightly different flavor—somewhere between cauliflower and broccoli. Rest assured *you* won't turn green when you eat it.

CAULIFLOWER BAKE

1 head cauliflower
3 tablespoons olive oil
1 large onion, sliced thin
Salt and pepper
¼ cup fine bread crumbs
¼ cup grated cheese (your favorite type)

Boil or steam cauliflower till almost tender. (Cook for ⅔ normal time.) Drain.

Heat oil in a skillet. Add onions and sauté till golden. Pour in crumbs. Stir until oil is evenly absorbed.

Place cauliflower (whole or in flowerets) in baking dish. Fold over it crumb-onion mixture. Season with salt and pepper and sprinkle cheese over top.

Put under broiler until cheese melts and top turns light brown.

Serves 4

CREAMED CAULIFLOWER

2 heads cauliflower, flowerets only, firm-cooked
2 tablespoons butter
2 tablespoons flour
1½ cups half and half or milk
2 tablespoons dry white wine (optional)
¼ lb. Blue cheese
Salt and pepper
Dash Tabasco sauce
Minced celery

Drain cauliflower. Make white sauce with butter, flour, and milk. Crumble cheese and add to sauce. Stir until melted. Season. Add wine, if desired.

Combine cauliflower and sauce, simmer briefly. Pour into serving dish. Garnish with minced celery.

Serves 6 to 8

CELERY

I'm sorry, but I just can't get worked up about celery.

I hope I haven't offended anyone, but you wouldn't want me to be dishonest, would you? And besides, I suspect the credibility of anybody who loves everything.

Celery *is* good for you, and when it's nice and fresh and crunchy and well-scrubbed and cold and the tops and very bottoms are

Use celery instead of a spoon.

trimmed off, it's not real bad. In fact, it's good. It's just not good enough to get worked up over, that's all.

Which doesn't mean I don't use it instead of a spoon to hold dips and various smooth cheeses or that I don't like a bowl of really well-prepared celery soup. It's just that I can't get worked up about celery.

Try these recipes. They're the very best I've come across. For them, I can *almost* get worked up. Maybe you can too.

CREAMED CELERY AND CHESTNUTS

4 cups sliced celery
3 cups water
1 teaspoon salt
½ cup (1 stick) butter or margarine
¼ cup flour
1 cup light cream
8 oz. mushrooms, sliced
1 11-oz. can whole chestnuts, drained
Salt, pepper, cayenne
1½ cups ½-inch bread cubes

Cook celery in salted water in covered saucepan. When tender but still crisp, drain and reserve 1 cup liquid.

Melt ¼ cup butter, stir in flour. Gradually stir in celery liquid and cream. Cook over low heat, stirring constantly, until mixture bubbles and thickens. Simmer sauce over low heat while stirring for 5 minutes. Lightly sauté mushrooms in a small amount of butter.

Stir in celery, mushrooms, and chestnuts. Season to taste with salt, pepper, and cayenne. Cook until ingredients are thoroughly heated.

Pour mixture into serving dish. Sauté bread cubes in remaining butter until golden. Sprinkle croutons over vegetables and serve.

Serves 8 to 10

CELERY BAKE

½ cup celery, chopped fine
½ cup onion, chopped fine
2 tablespoons walnuts, chopped fine
¾ cup tomato juice
1 tablespoon grated Cheddar cheese
Salt
1 tablespoon melted butter
¾ cup whole wheat bread crumbs
2 eggs
Oil

Combine celery, onion, and walnuts with tomato juice, Cheddar cheese, a pinch of salt, melted butter, and all but 2 tablespoons of the bread crumbs.

Beat 2 eggs and blend into the mixture. Oil a cake or loaf pan and place remaining bread crumbs on the base. Spoon in mixture and bake at 375° for 30 to 35 minutes.

Serves 4 to 6

BRAISED CELERY WITH ALMONDS

2 tablespoons chopped onion
2½ cups celery, cut into ½-inch diagonal slices
2 tablespoons butter or margarine
1 teaspoon vegetable-seasoned stock base
⅓ cup warm water
¼ cup toasted slivered almonds
Salt

Cook onions and celery in butter slowly until slightly golden. Stir the stock base into water. Add to vegetable mixture. Cover and cook until celery is tender and liquid is absorbed. Add almonds and salt to taste. Toss lightly. Serve at once.

Serves 4 to 5

CORN

Some of you may think that some of this book's been corny—well, lend me your ears 'cause you ain't heard nothin' yet!

Now I'm *really* going to get corny, as I present to you the one truly American vegetable.

That's right—when the Pilgrims landed at Plymouth Rock they were amazed to see the colorful Maize (corn) which was the principal vegetable in the diet of the American Indian.

The One Truly American Vegetable.

Actually, corn comes in several varieties, one of which is not grown for consumption but for decoration and is known, rather uninventively, as Ornamental Corn—or "Rainbow Corn." You'll find this variety with its brightly colored kernels of red, orange, yellow, blue, or black in your supermarket around Thanksgiving and Christmas time; piled in a basket with some ornamental gourds, it lends a festive look to your kitchen table.

The major corn crop—the kind we buy, cook, and eat right off the cob or simmered in a cream sauce is called sweet corn. (There are two varieties, one much yellower than the other—just a mite tougher and not as sweet as its almost white brother.)

Corn, among all the vegetables—and this is important—is probably better brought frozen than fresh, because when corn is picked, the sugar changes to starch very quickly. Only by racing straight from field to boiling water can you really get corn's full taste and nutritional value.

However, the traditional "corn-on-the-cob" is delicious with butter and seasoning, so every now and then you simply have to give a little to get a little.

Corn is also the only cereal crop that home gardeners are likely to grow. If you live in a warm to mild climate zone and have some reasonably large backyard space, you should have no trouble reaping a good healthy harvest. Plant seeds deeply in good, rich soil right about the beginning of spring. Be sure to make short, compact rows so that the pollen will blow into all ears and insure full, thick rows of kernels. Water frequently, and prepare to harvest about a month after the silk appears at the top of the ears. The juice from the kernels should be milky as opposed to watery, and a too-thick consistency means you've waited too long.

Naturally, you can make popcorn from the dried kernels, and also quite naturally you can make the following corn dishes from the recipes listed below.

Oh, incidentally. It might be helpful to know that three ears of corn yield about one cup of kernels; six ears of grated corn yield about one cup of kernels; one package frozen cut corn yields about two cups kernels. And of course, one fried chicken stand yields one kernel.

Forgive me. I simply couldn't control myself.

CORN FRITTERS

1 egg, beaten
½ cup milk
2 cups corn kernels
1½ cups sifted flour
2 teaspoons baking powder
1 teaspoon salt
¼ teaspoon pepper
1 tablespoon melted butter
Vegetable oil for deep frying
Honey

Combine the egg, milk, and corn. Sift together the flour, baking powder, and salt; add to corn mixture and beat well. Stir in pepper and melted butter

Heat the fat to 375°. Drop the batter into it by the tablespoon and fry until golden brown. Drain on absorbent paper. Serve with honey.

Serves 4 to 6.

FRESH CORN PUDDING

16 to 18 ears very fresh corn (enough for 3 cups pulp)
1 egg, separated
2 teaspoons sugar
1 teaspoon salt
3 tablespoons butter or margarine

With a sharp knife slit down center of each row of corn kernels. With dull edge of knife press out pulp and juice into a bowl. Add egg yolk, sugar, salt, and 2 tablespoons melted butter.

Beat egg white until stiff peaks form; fold into corn mixture. Turn into greased shallow 1-quart baking dish and dot with remaining butter. Bake at 350° for 45 minutes or until golden brown.

Serves 6

CORN CHOWDER

2 tablespoons butter or margarine
¼ cup coarsely chopped onion
1½ cups boiling water
2 cups peeled, diced potatoes
1 teaspoon salt
¼ teaspoon pepper
3 cups fresh corn kernels cut off the cob (about 9 ears)
3½ cups milk
Paprika

In a 3-quart saucepan melt the butter. Add onion and cook until soft. Add boiling water, potatoes, salt and pepper; cook covered over moderate heat for 10 minutes, until potatoes are almost tender.

Add corn and milk and cook uncovered 10 minutes more, until heated through. Do not allow soup to boil.

Sprinkle paprika on soup before serving.

Serves 4

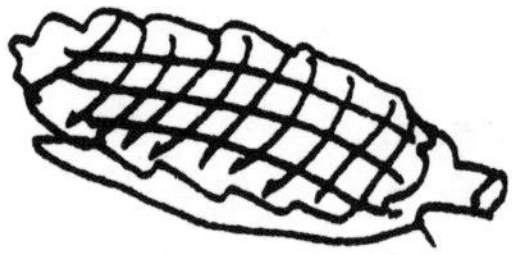

CUCUMBER

I used to think that the height of snobbery was serving little cucumber sandwiches. Then one day I went to a party where they served them, ate a couple, and now I don't think I'd ever have a party without them!

Well, perhaps an exaggeration—but the cucumber, which is a member of the gourd family, is truly delicious as a raw vegetable, as a snack, or in a salad. Besides the most traditional dill pickles, cucumbers can get into all manners of other pickles, too: Gherkins, Bread and Butter . . .

Here, to help you out of *your* pickle as to what to do with those rich-green firm shiny cucumbers, are some recipes, including those for the above.

I used to think that the height of snobbery was serving little cucumber sandwiches.

CREAM CHEESE AND CUCUMBER SANDWICHES

Slender sourdough bread
or
Pressed pumpernickel bread
Cream cheese (or sweet butter)
Cucumber
Salt
Paprika

Cut thin slices from a sourdough baguette, or cut slices of square pressed pumpernickel into quarters.

Spread each slice with cream cheese. Score a large, firm cucumber with a fork to give it a pretty pattern and slice it about ⅛- to ¼-inch thick. Put a slice of cucumber in the center of each sandwich and salt it very lightly. Then sprinkle some paprika down the center of the sandwich for decoration.

CRISP CUCUMBER SALAD

2 medium cucumbers (about 1 lb., peeled and sliced thin
1 small onion, sliced thin
½ cup sour cream
2 tablespoons sugar
3 tablespoons cider vinegar
¾ teaspoon salt
¼ teaspoon dry mustard
¼ teaspoon pepper
1 tablespoon minced parsley

In serving dish gently toss cucumbers and onions to mix. Chill until serving time.

Beat sour cream, sugar, vinegar, salt, mustard, and pepper until well blended. Pour over cucumber-onion mixture; sprinkle with parsley. Serve at once.

Serves 4 to 6

BREAD 'N BUTTER PICKLES

2 quarts medium cucumbers
4 large onions
1 green pepper
¼ cup coarse salt
2½ cups sugar
¾ teaspoon turmeric
¼ teaspoon ground cloves
1 tablespoon white mustard seed
½ teaspoon celery seed
3½ cups vinegar

Cut unpeeled cucumbers into thin slices. Peel onions and slice thinly. Cut pepper in half, remove seeds, and cut into narrow strips.

Combine cucumbers, onions, pepper, and sprinkle with coarse salt. Let stand 3 hours.

Rinse off salt with cold water and drain thoroughly. Combine sugar, turmeric, cloves, mustard seed, and vinegar in large preserving kettle. Heat to scalding, stirring to dissolve sugar. Add drained vegetables to hot pickling liquid and heat just to boiling.

Seal at once in sterilized jars.

Makes 6 pints

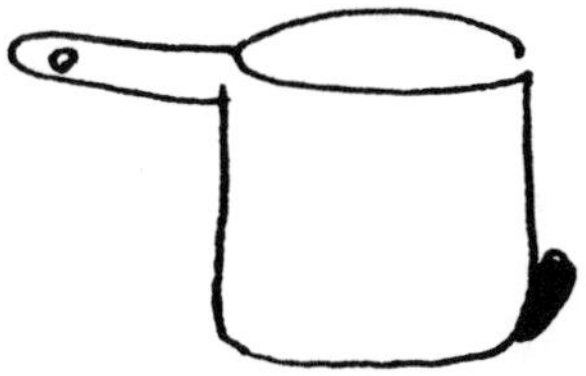

DILL PICKLES

30 cucumbers
½ cup coarse salt
2 quarts water
2 tablespoons vinegar
4 cloves garlic
4 bay leaves
¼ teaspoon mustard seed
1 teaspoon mixed pickling spice
10 sprigs dill

Buy even-sized cucumbers and be sure they are very firm. Wash and dry them. Arrange the cucumbers in a crock or jar.

Bring the salt and water to a boil. Cool, then add the vinegar, garlic, bay leaves, mustard seed, and pickling spice.

Pour over the cucumbers. Arrange the dill over all. The liquid should completely cover the cucumbers; if not, add more salted water.

If crock is used, cover with a plate or wooden board to weight it down. Loosely cover with cheesecloth. Keep in a cool place for a week. If you like very green pickles, you might test one at the end of 5 days.

EGGPLANT

I have always liked eggplant.

But I never *loved* eggplant until one summer when I found out just how many needs an eggplant could fill.

Let me tell you a quick story of how a love for a vegetable and a great recipe were born. It will help you see how easily you can make up your own recipes once you start thinking cooking.

I was visiting a friend's home and as the warm, summer day drew toward evening, he suggested having a barbecue. Out came a bunch of steaks, and only after the coals were burning a soft red glow and the marinated steaks had been thrust upon the grill did he realize I did not eat meat and something would have to be done about it. In a flash of inspiration, I asked him if he had an eggplant. He did. I went into the house, cut two inch-thick slices of the eggplant, and hustled them out to the barbecue where I marinated them in the same sauce as the

Everybody else wanted some eggplant today.

steaks, grilled them, then hustled them back into the house where I topped them each with a thick slice of beefsteak tomato, a fat mushroom, put them under the broiler for a couple of minutes, whipped up some Bearnaise sauce, and rejoiced at the birth of "Eggplant Tournedos."

The only problem was that once the other guests tasted them, everybody wanted some, so I wound up having to cook for my supper.

You all know that envy or possessiveness is not in my nature, so you will not be surprised that I'm about to share some secrets of my love with you.

EGGPLANT CAVIAR

2 medium eggplants
2 cloves garlic, minced
1 large tomato, chopped
½ cup finely chopped scallions
½ cup finely chopped black olives
⅛ cup wine vinegar
⅛ cup lemon juice
¼ cup olive oil
Salt and pepper

Bake unpeeled eggplants in oven at 350° for 2 hours or until really soft. Cool. Split eggplants lengthwise. If the seeds are dark brown and starting to separate from the rest of the eggplant, they will be bitter—discard.

Chop pulp and combine with next 4 ingredients. Blend vinegar, lemon juice, olive oil, and salt and pepper to taste. Toss with eggplant mixture and chill.

Serve as appetizer with crackers or pita bread.

Makes approximately 4 cups

TOFU-EGGPLANT CASSEROLE

1 medium eggplant, cut in ½-inch round slices, unpeeled
Salt and pepper
Flour
Oil
1 medium onion, diced
½ lb. tomatoes, chopped
8 to 10 oz. drained tofu
1 15-oz. can tomato sauce
¼ cup unsalted sunflower seeds
1 teaspoon minced garlic
½ teaspoon oregano
½ teaspoon basil
1 cup cottage cheese
1 egg
1½ cups shredded Mozzarella cheese
¾ cup soft whole wheat bread crumbs

Sprinkle each slice of eggplant on both sides with salt and pepper. Dredge in flour. Heat about ¼ inch oil in large skillet over high heat. Fry eggplant on both sides until lightly browned. Drain on paper.

Sauté onion in 2 tablespoons oil for 2 minutes. Add tomatoes, tofu, tomato sauce, sunflower seeds, garlic, oregano, basil, and salt and pepper to taste. Combine cottage cheese, egg, and ¼ cup Mozzarella cheese.

Arrange eggplant slices on bottom of 9-inch square baking dish or other shallow casserole. Spread with half of the cottage cheese mixture and half of the tofu sauce. Repeat. Sprinkle top with remaining Mozzarella cheese and bread crumbs. Bake at 350° for 30 minutes.

Serves 4 to 6

EGGPLANT TERIYAKI

1 lb. Italian eggplant (about 4 to 6)
Vegetable or sesame oil
¼ cup soy sauce
¼ cup sake or sauterne
¼ cup sugar
1 tablespoon grated fresh ginger
Toasted sesame seeds

Slice eggplant 1 inch thick. Soak in water 10 to 15 minutes. Drain and dry.

Heat heavy skillet. Add vegetable or sesame oil. Cook both sides of eggplant in oil until soft and tender. Remove from heat.

Mix soy sauce, sake, sugar, ginger, and a few drops of sesame oil. Add to eggplant and let marinate 10 to 20 minutes before serving. Sprinkle with sesame seeds. Serve hot or at room temperature.

Serves 6

CHEESE-STUFFED EGGPLANT ROLLS

2 medium eggplants
Salt
1 cup olive oil
8 oz. Ricotta cheese
8 oz. Mozzarella cheese, diced
1 oz. Romano or Parmesan cheese
1 egg, beaten
1 tablespoon minced parsley
Pepper
Tomato sauce

Peel eggplants and cut lengthwise into ½-inch slices. Sprinkle with 1 teaspoon salt and stack the slices on plate. Place a weighted object on eggplant and let stand 1 hour, then drain. Dry eggplant with paper towels.

Heat oil in skillet, add eggplant, and sauté until lightly browned.

Combine Ricotta, Mozzarella, ½ oz. Romano, egg, parsley, salt and pepper to taste, and mix well. Put 1 tablespoon of cheese mixture on each eggplant slice and roll. Place in a 13 × 9 × 2-inch baking pan, seam side down. Spoon tomato sauce over rolls and sprinkle with remaining ½ oz. Romano cheese. Bake at 350° for 20 minutes.

Serves 8

EGGPLANT PARMESAN

1 large eggplant (about 1½ lb.)
2 eggs, slightly beaten
1½ cups fine dry seasoned bread crumbs
½ to 1 cup olive oil
2 15-oz. cans tomato sauce
1½ teaspoons dried oregano leaves
½ teaspoon salt
1½ lb. Mozzarella cheese, thinly sliced
1 cup grated Parmesan cheese

Pare and slice eggplant crosswise into ¼-inch slices. Dip slices into beaten eggs and then the bread crumbs, making sure to coat each slice completely.

Heat enough oil to cover the bottom of a large skillet over moderate heat. Fry eggplant slices, a few at a time, until browned on both sides. Add more oil to the skillet as needed. Drain slices well on paper towels.

In a well-greased, shallow, 8-inch square baking dish, layer ⅓ of the eggplant slices, ⅓ of the tomato sauce, ⅓ of the oregano, ⅓ of the salt, ⅓ of the Parmesan cheese, and ⅓ of the Mozzarella cheese. Repeat layers twice more, ending with the Mozzarella.

Bake uncovered at 350° for 25 to 30 minutes, until sauce is hot and cheeses have melted.

Serves 4 to 6

STUFFED EGGPLANT

1 medium eggplant, cut in half lengthwise
Water
Salt and pepper
7 slices bread, dried
2 eggs
1 small onion, chopped
2 to 3 stalks celery, chopped
¼ cup catsup
½ teaspoon mustard
Pat of butter

With paring knife, remove pulp from eggplant. Leave ⅛ inch meat in the shell. Slice meat. Put in pan over small flame, adding 1 tablespoon of water and pinch of salt. Steam until tender, approximately 10 minutes.

Crumble dried bread into bowl. Add 2 eggs, salt and pepper to taste, onion, celery, mashed-up eggplant, and a pat of butter. Mix in mustard and catsup. Return to eggplant shell. Bake at 350° for 1 hour.

Serves 2

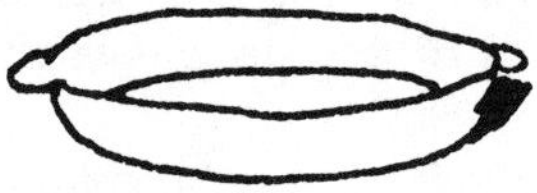

GREEN PEPPERS

There are two kinds of peppers (three if you include Dr.)—the sweet and the hot.

We have come to talk of the sweet variety, which is truly magical in that, if you wait long enough, it'll turn from green to red. These peppers, which remain mild even when red, are the kind you use for stuffing and salads. Hot peppers range from pea-size to a long, narrow variety, but all are pungent and range from hot to hotter to hottest.

When buying your sweet green peppers (also called bell peppers), be sure they are large, firm, and shiny, any tinge of red is okay. Like all vegetables, they should be bought before they begin to soften.

Prior to stuffing peppers, you should boil them for five or six minutes until they are almost—but not quite—tender. (Save the liquid for sauces or stocks.) Then slice off the tops and remove the seeds.

If you wait long enough the peppers will change from green to red.

Peppers should be sliced raw when added to salads, lightly stir-fried before adding to omelets, and a real taste treat can be devised by placing a raw pepper right on the flame of your stove, waiting until the outer shell is burnt, then removing the burnt skin and eating what's left.

You can stuff peppers with almost anything.

RICE-STUFFED PEPPERS

4 green peppers
2 cups whole wheat bread crumbs
1 cup boiled brown rice
1 tablespoon seedless raisins
¾ cup chopped mushrooms
2 tablespoons tomato puree
Salt and pepper
2 tablespoons chopped onion (optional)
Butter or margarine

Fry the mushrooms (and onions if used) for a few minutes. Then add the remaining ingredients except the peppers.

Keep over low heat while you slice the peppers in half lengthwise, remove the seeds, and wash in cold water. Spoon the fried mixture into the pepper halves and dot with butter.

Place the peppers in a baking dish and bake at 350° until peppers are soft, about 40 to 45 minutes. If desired, a little grated cheese may be added to the top of each pepper about 8 minutes before removing from oven.

Serves 4

POTATO-CHEESE STUFFED PEPPERS

6 green peppers
Boiling water
1½ teaspoons salt
3 tablespoons finely chopped onion
¼ teaspoon minced garlic
3 cups diced cooked potatoes
1 cup diced Cheddar cheese
½ cup chopped celery
¼ teaspoon pepper
½ cup soft bread crumbs
Butter or margarine

Wash peppers. Cut thin slice from stem end and remove seeds. Place peppers in saucepan with boiling water to cover and 1 teaspoon salt. Cover, bring to boil, boil 5 minutes. Remove from water and invert to drain well.

Cook onion and garlic in 2 tablespoons butter until tender. Add potatoes, cheese, celery, ½ teaspoon salt, and pepper. Mix well and spoon into peppers.

Mix bread crumbs and 1 tablespoon butter. Sprinkle over tops of peppers. Place in casserole. Cover and bake at 350° for 30 minutes. Uncover and bake 10 minutes longer to brown bread crumbs.

Serves 6

LEEKS

Obviously, in this book when we talk about "fixing a leek" we don't mean calling the plumber, we mean calling the cook.

Leeks are a member of the onion family and look like fat scallions. If you don't know what a scallion looks like, it's sort of a skinny leek.

There really isn't a whole lot to say about leeks other than their taste is a bit more delicate than an onion and most people don't know what to do with them. So, in an effort to be helpful, here are a couple of recipes which will help find the leeks in your vegetable cookery.

By the way. Leeks are the "pigpens" of the vegetable family. Somehow they manage to gather more dirt and grit in the deep crevices of their leaves than almost anything. So split them part way and rinse out all the dirt.

In fact, when you call the cook, perhaps you'd better call the bottle washer.

Leeks taste a bit more delicate than onion.

LEEK PIE

10 leeks, cleaned and sliced in 1-inch pieces, green-leaves removed
½ cup vegetable bouillon
Juice of ½ lemon
2 tablespoons butter
2 tablespoons dry sherry
4 eggs
¼ cup heavy cream
2 cups Ricotta or dry curd cottage cheese
Bread crumbs
Salt to taste

Simmer leeks in bouillon, lemon juice, butter, and sherry for 12 to 15 minutes, until tender.

Beat together 1 egg and cream. Add ½ cup hot cooking liquid to egg mixture gradually, stirring constantly. Slowly pour onto leeks and blend well. Simmer for a few moments to thicken cream. Beat 3 eggs well, add Ricotta cheese. Mix with leeks and sauce.

Grease a pie plate. Dust plate with bread crumbs. Add leak-egg mixture. Bake at 375° about 40 minutes or until set.

Serves 4 to 6

LEEK SALAD

1 lb. leeks
1 large grapefruit
French dressing
Lettuce

Wash leeks in running water, cut off green tops and bottom roots. Tie together and cook covered in boiling water for 20 to 30 minutes. Drain and chill thoroughly.

Peel and section grapefruit. Cut sections into halves and toss with leeks. Add French dressing. Serve on a bed of lettuce.

Serves 4 to 6.

MUSHROOMS

As Mr. Mother Earth, the Plant Expert, I am often asked if there is any plant that will grow in the dark. My answer—mushrooms.

In spite of the fact that mushrooms are fungi and many are toxic and thus inedible (these are usually called toadstools), they are also a delicious and integral part of vegetable cookery.

It is most important that you *buy* your mushrooms as opposed to

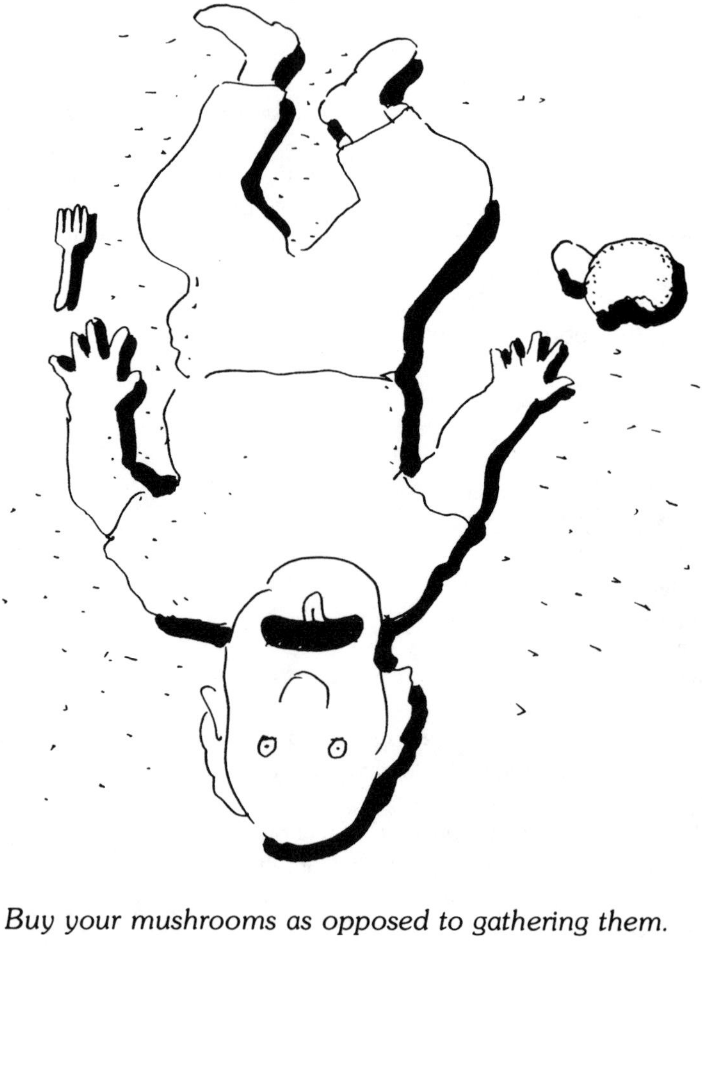

Buy your mushrooms as opposed to gathering them.

trying to gather them yourself, because unless you are an expert it's difficult to know which can be eaten and which cannot.

Mushrooms have almost no calories and are marvelous in soups, salads, omelets—practically any vegetable dish. The other night I mixed some lightly fried mushrooms and onions with some melted Cheddar cheese, a healthy dash or three of Worcestershire sauce, some crumbled-up pumpernickel, and a few slices of tomato and came out with a delicious mushroom-cheese casserole.

When buying your mushrooms, make sure they are light-colored, unmottled, and firm with creamy white undersides. The gills should not be exposed—if they are, you're looking at an old mushroom. Beware of wetness, dark spots, and splotches. There's no point in buying a fungus with a fungus.

Even though mushrooms grow in the dark, there's no reason to keep you in the dark any longer about mushroom cookery.

So . . .

MUSHROOMS MARINARA

1 lb. fresh mushrooms
4 tablespoons olive oil
2 teaspoons lemon juice
¼ teaspoon minced garlic
2 teaspoons parsley flakes
¼ teaspoon ground black pepper
1 teaspoon salt
¼ teaspoon oregano leaves

Rinse, pat dry, and slice fresh mushrooms. This makes about 5 cups.

Heat oil in large skillet with lemon juice and minced garlic. Add mushrooms. Saute 5 to 7 minutes or until tender. Blend in remaining ingredients. Serve hot.

Great over spaghetti.

Serves 4

MARINATED MUSHROOMS

¾ lb. fresh mushrooms
6 tablespoons olive oil
3 tablespoons white vinegar
1 teaspoon oregano leaves
1 teaspoon salt
½ teaspoon sugar
¼ teaspoon ground black pepper
¼ cup finely chopped onion
2 tablespoons diced pimento
½ clove garlic, minced

Rinse, pat dry, and trim stems of fresh mushrooms. Drop into boiling water for 1 minute, then drain, immerse in ice water until completely chilled, and drain thoroughly.

In a small bowl, combine oil, vinegar, oregano, salt, sugar, and black pepper. Mix well. Stir in onion, pimento, and garlic. Alternately spoon mushrooms and oil-vinegar mixture into quart jar. Cover and chill thoroughly.

Serve as an appetizer or side dish. These mushrooms keep several weeks refrigerated.

Makes 1 quart

BAKED MUSHROOMS AND NOODLES

½ lb. fresh mushrooms
1 tablespoon butter or margarine
½ cup finely diced onions
1 clove garlic, minced
3 cups fine noodles
1/16 teaspoon ground black pepper
1 cup creamed cottage cheese
1 cup sour cream
1 teaspoon Worcestershire sauce
½ teaspoon salt
Paprika

Rinse, pat dry, and slice fresh mushrooms (makes 2½ cups).

Heat butter in skillet. Add mushrooms, onion, and garlic. Sauté 4 to 5 minutes.

Cook noodles in boiling salted water until tender. Drain.

Combine the cottage cheese, sour cream, Worcestershire sauce, and salt and pepper in a bowl. Add the mushrooms and noodles to this mixture. Spoon into a greased 10 × 6 × 2-inch baking dish. Bake at 350° for 30 minutes, or until bubbly. Garnish with paprika before serving.

Serves 6

MUSHROOM BURGER

1 lb. mushrooms
½ cup salted peanuts
1½ small onions
8 slices whole wheat bread
2 eggs, lightly beaten
¾ teaspoon salt
½ teaspoon curry powder
¼ teaspoon pepper
¼ cup oil

Shred or chop mushrooms, peanuts, and onions, and make bread crumbs, using grater or food processor. Combine in bowl. Add eggs, salt, curry powder, and pepper. Mix well.

Shape into patties about 3 inches in diameter.

In large skillet, heat oil until hot. Add patties, fry over moderate heat until golden, about 4 minutes on each side.

Serve in warm, whole wheat pita pockets or on English muffin halves with lettuce and cheese, if desired.

Makes 8 patties

STUFFED MUSHROOMS AMANDINE

12 large mushrooms
½ cup toasted chopped almonds
¼ cup shredded cheese
½ cup tartar sauce
2 tablespoons chopped green onion
Salt

Wash mushrooms, cut off stems, and arrange cup sides up in shallow baking dish.

Trim and chop stems. Mix chopped stems with ¼ cup almonds, cheese, tartar sauce, onion, and salt to taste. Spoon into mushroom caps. Top with remaining almonds and bake at 425° for 8 to 10 minutes. Serve hot.

Serves 6

MUSHROOMS PAPRIKA

1 lb. fresh mushrooms
3 tablespoons margarine or butter
2 small onions, chopped
1 teaspoon salt
¼ teaspoon fresh black pepper
½ teaspoon paprika
2 tablespoons heavy cream
¼ cup sour cream
Toast

Clean mushrooms. Slice, leaving on stems

Melt margarine in skillet. Add onions; cook over low heat, stirring frequently, until golden. Add mushrooms, salt, and pepper. Cover; simmer over low heat, stirring occasionally until tender (8 to 10 minutes). Stir in paprika. Remove from heat.

When ready to serve, stir in heavy cream, then sour cream. Heat, but do not boil. Serve on toast.

Serves 4

MUSHROOM LOAF

2 lb. mushrooms
3 tablespoons butter or margarine
1 small onion, minced
4 eggs
⅓ cup milk
1½ cups fine dry bread crumbs
1½ teaspoons salt
1 teaspoon marjoram, crushed
⅛ teaspoon pepper
4 hard-cooked eggs, coarsely chopped

Rinse and pat dry mushrooms. Finely chop 1½ lb. of the mushrooms (makes about 6 cups). Set aside. Slice remaining mushrooms (makes about 2 cups).

In small skillet melt 2 tablespoons butter. Add sliced mushrooms, sauté until tender, about 5 minutes. Remove with slotted spoon and set aside to use as garnish. Melt remaining 1 tablespoon butter. Add onion, sauté until tender, about 5 minutes.

In a large mixing bowl lightly beat eggs. Add milk, 1¼ cup bread crumbs, salt, marjoram, pepper, sauteed onions, and chopped mushrooms. Stir until mixture is well blended and smooth. Stir in hard-cooked eggs.

Butter a 9 × 5-inch loaf pan. Coat pan with remaining ¼ cup bread crumbs. Spoon mixture evenly into pan. Cover pan with greased foil. Bake at 375° until firm, about 1½ hours. Loosen edges with spatula, invert onto serving platter.

In small skillet, heat reserved sliced mushrooms. Use to garnish top of loaf.

Serves 6

ONIONS

A friend of mine is so proud of her delicious hot cheese, bread, and egg-top onion soup she's asked that her epitaph read: "She really knew her onions."

By the time you finish this book, you'll really know *your* onions, an integrated family if there ever was one: They come in white, yellow, red, brown . . . unfortunately, in the onion family, black isn't beautiful, it's rotten. . . .

"L'oignon est le roi des legumes."

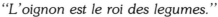

You will also get to know all of the onion's nieces and nephews—the leeks, the shallots, the garlics—a real fun group, I assure you.

You'll probably know more about onions than you really need to know, like onions are all members of the lily family.

Great French chefs have been heard to say "*L'oignon est le roi des legumes*"—the onion is the king of vegetables. The fact is, onion and its relatives are absolutely indispensable to good—even bad—cooking.

Whether you prefer the strong white onion, the milder Bermuda onion, or the in-between Spanish or Red Onions—whether you prefer scallions or leeks or shallots—it matters not.

Add any form of onion to just about any form of food and it's bound to taste better.

In fact, I'm convinced the only reason *I* cry while slicing onions is because I love and respect them so much.

CREAMED ONION SOUP

4 tablespoons butter
4 cups thinly sliced onions
1 tablespoon flour
1½ quarts water
2 teaspoons salt
¼ teaspoon white pepper
2 egg yolks
1 cup heavy cream
Grated Gruyere or Parmesan cheese

Melt the butter in a saucepan. Sauté the onions over low heat about 20 minutes, until browned. Mix in the flour and sauté another 5 minutes. Add the water, salt, and pepper. Cover loosely and cook over low heat 25 minutes.

Beat the egg yolks and cream in a bowl. Gradually add about 3 cups of the soup, stirring steadily to prevent curdling. Return to balance of soup. Heat, mixing steadily, but do not let boil.

Serve with a bowl of grated cheese.

Serves 6 to 8

ONION PIE

1 baked 9-inch pie shell
4 cups chopped onions
2 tablespoons butter
2 tablespoons olive oil
½ teaspoon salt
¼ teaspoon pepper
2 cups shredded Swiss cheese
2 tablespoons sliced ripe olives
2 tablespoons grated Parmesan cheese
2 teaspoons chopped parsley

Sauté onions in butter and olive oil just until tender and translucent. Season with salt and pepper. Place half the Swiss cheese in bottom of pie shell. Top with half the onions. Repeat layers. Sprinkle olives and Parmesan cheese over top. Bake at 350° for 20 minutes. Serve hot.

Serves 6

ONION-CUCUMBER SALAD

2 onions
2 cucumbers
½ cup cider vinegar
¼ cup water
1 teaspoon sugar
1 teaspoon salt
¼ teaspoon freshly ground black pepper

Peel the onions and cucumbers. Cut into paper-thin slices. Cover with salted ice water. Cover and chill for 3 to 4 hours. Drain. Add the vinegar, water, sugar, salt and pepper.

Serves 4 to 6

NUTTED ONION CUPS

6 large onions
Water, salt
½ cup butter or margarine, melted
2 cups bread stuffing mix
¼ cup minced parsley
½ teaspoon garlic salt
½ cup chopped walnuts

Peel onions and cut a thin slice from root end of each so they will stand level. Cut a slice from top of each onion.

Using a skewer, pierce each onion several times from top through center to prevent them from collapsing while cooking. Stand onions upright in a saucepan in which they fit snugly, adding boiling water to a depth of 2 inches, and salt lightly. Cover and bring to a boil. Reduce heat and cook 30 to 35 minutes, until onions are tender but not mushy. Cool and scoop out centers.

Chop centers and set aside. Brush onion cups with melted butter.

Combine stuffing mix, chopped onions, remaining melted butter, parsley, garlic salt, and walnuts. Pile into onion cups. Arrange in a greased shallow baking dish and bake at 325° for 35 minutes.

Serves 6

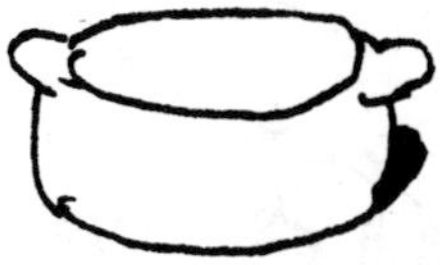

PEAS

"They are alike as two peas in a pod . . ."

How often have we heard that expression? The only thing is, I don't get it. Every pea in every pod is different from every other pea in the entire pea world, but they are pretty much alike in that they taste terrific.

Ever eat raw peas? Bet you haven't! Well, you ought to give it a try. I'm not sure whether I like the smell of Sweet Peas the Flower more or the taste of Sweet Peas the Vegetable.

I'm not sure whether I like the smell of Sweet Peas the Flower more or Sweet Peas the Vegetable.

Besides the traditional boiled peas with butter, you can steam or stir-fry peas in their shells (this is particularly effective with Chinese peas which are more pod than pea), you can use them in cold vegetable salads, or you can use them in any of the recipes included below.

Be prepared for some surprises. For instance, there might be a thousand different recipes for pea soup, but no two pea soups ever taste alike. You might say they're as different as two peas in a pod.

FRENCH PEAS

8 large lettuce leaves, washed
2 lb. peas, shelled
2 tablespoons thinly sliced scallions
½ teaspoon sugar
½ teaspoon salt
⅛ teaspoon pepper
⅛ teaspoon dried chervil
⅛ teaspoon dried thyme leaves
2 tablespoons butter or margarine

Cover bottom and sides of a 10-inch skillet with 4 of the moist lettuce leaves. Top with peas and sprinkle with green onions, sugar, salt, pepper, chervil, and thyme, and dot with butter. Cover peas with remaining lettuce leaves.

Cover skillet tightly and cook over low heat for 10 to 15 minutes, until peas are tender. Remove lettuce leaves. Toss peas well before serving.

Serves 4

SPLIT PEA SOUP

1 lb. green split peas
3 quarts water
1½ teaspoons salt
2½ tablespoons butter
1½ cups finely chopped carrots
1 cup finely chopped sweet potato
1 cup finely chopped onions
½ cup finely chopped celery
½ to ¾ teaspoon ground marjoram
1 teaspoon dried basil
1 to 2 cloves garlic, minced
½ to ¾ teaspoon ground cumin
½ cup dry white wine
Fresh ground black pepper to taste
Croutons

Put the split peas in a large pot with the water and salt. Bring the water to a boil, then lower the heat and simmer for about 1 hour. Skim off the foam from the top and discard it.

Sauté the finely chopped carrots, sweet potato, onions, and celery in the butter for about 10 minutes, stirring constantly. Add the herbs and cook the vegetables for another 5 minutes, then add them to the soup.

Simmer the soup, stirring occasionally, for an hour.

Ladle out approximately half the soup and puree it in a blender. Return the puree to the pot. Add the wine and pepper, stir, and bring the soup back to a simmer.

Serve hot, alone or with croutons.

Serves 6 to 8

OLD-FASHIONED CREAMED PEAS

2 cups fresh peas
4 lettuce leaves
¼ teaspoon chervil or marjoram
¼ teaspoon salt
¼ cup water
2 oz. butter
1 egg yolk
¼ cup half and half or cream
½ teaspoon sugar
Dash pepper

Place lettuce at bottom of saucepan. Add water, herbs, seasonings, peas, and butter. Bring to a boil, reduce heat and simmer, covered, until tender.

Remove lettuce and discard. Mix in cream mixed with yolk, sugar, and pepper. Pour into serving dish.

Serves 4

POTATOES

I think potatoes have taken their lumps long enough. (There is a pun in there—but you have to dig for it just like you have to dig for potatoes, which are a tuberous root.)

Sure, potatoes are good boiled or baked or fried or in a potato salad or mashed or made into potato pancakes or soups.

You'll never know the true joys a potato can bring.

By adding any number of seasonings such as garlic or onion or dill or sage, by sprinkling with grated Cheddar or Parmesan cheese, by stuffing with sour cream and chives, you can turn a baked potato into a feast for the gods. (Please remember never to throw away the potato peel—it's the most nutritious part of this vegetable and can even be eaten all by its lonesome, delicious fried in beer batter.)

But unless you have the recipes for the pancakes and the soups and a couple of other good things, you'll never know the true joys a potato can bring.

I think that after you've tried these potato delights, you'll know there's more to a potato than meets its eyes.

POTATO LATKES (PANCAKES)

2 eggs
3 cups grated, drained potatoes
4 tablespoons grated onion
1 teaspoon salt
¼ teaspoon pepper
2 tablespoons cracker or matzo meal
½ cup fat or butter
Applesauce or sour cream

Beat the eggs and add the potatoes, onion, salt, pepper, and cracker or matzo meal.

Heat half the fat or butter in a skillet. When fat is sizzling, drop the potato mixture into the pan by the tablespoon. Fry until browned on both sides. Keep pancakes hot until all are fried, and add more butter or fat as required.

Garnish with applesauce or sour cream.

Serves 8

POTATO SOUP

3 tablespoons butter
1 cup diced onions
3 cups cubed potatoes
1 grated carrot
3 cups water
2 teaspoons salt
½ teaspoon pepper
1 teaspoon caraway seeds (optional)
3 cups milk
3 tablespoons minced parsley
½ cup sour cream

Melt the butter in a saucepan and brown onions. Add the potatoes, carrot, water, salt, pepper, and caraway seeds. Bring to a boil, then cook over low heat 20 minutes. Stir in milk and parsley and bring back to boiling point.

Serve hot; garnish with sour cream.

Serves 6 to 8

POTATO KUGEL (PUDDING)

6 potatoes
1 onion, grated
2 egg yolks, beaten
4 tablespoons cracker or matzo meal
1 teaspoon baking powder
1½ teaspoons salt
¼ teaspoon freshly ground black pepper
4 tablespoons melted butter
2 egg whites, stiffly beaten

Peel and grate the potatoes into salted water. Drain the potatoes well. Combine in a bowl with the onion, egg yolks, cracker or matzo meal, baking powder, salt, pepper, and 2 tablespoons butter. Mix together well. Fold in the egg whites carefully but thoroughly.

Pour the mixture into a greased 1½-quart baking dish. Pour the remaining butter on top.

Bake in oven at 375° for 1 hour, or until the mixture is set and lightly browned on top. Chill and serve cold.

Serves 4 to 6 as main course, 10 to 12 as side dish.

POTATO PUFFS

5 cups mashed potatoes (approx. 2 lb.)
4 tablespoons melted butter
2 eggs, beaten
3 tablespoons flour
3 tablespoons grated onion
1 clove garlic, minced
2 tablespoons minced parsley
1½ teaspoons salt
¼ teaspoon white pepper
¼ teaspoon nutmeg

Beat together all the ingredients until light and fluffy. Drop by the heaping tablespoon onto a buttered baking pan.

Bake in a 375° oven for 10 minutes, or until browned. Serve with browned butter if desired.

Serves 6 to 8

GARDEN POTATO SALAD

2 lb. medium potatoes
3 hard-cooked eggs, sliced
½ cup chopped celery
¼ cup minced onion
¼ cup chopped green pepper
2 tablespoons chopped parsley
¾ cup mayonnaise
1 teaspoon salt
½ teaspoon dry mustard
¼ teaspoon pepper

Wash potatoes and cook in a small amount of boiling water until tender, about 30 minutes. Drain, let cool slightly. Peel potatoes and cut into ½-inch cubes.

In a large mixing bowl, combine potatoes with eggs, celery, onion, green pepper, parsley, mayonnaise, salt, mustard, and pepper. Serve well chilled.

Serves 6

HOT GERMAN POTATO SALAD

2 tablespoons butter or margarine
6 medium potatoes (2 lb.)
½ cup chopped onion
2 teaspoons sugar
2 teaspoons salt
1 teaspoon flour
⅛ teaspoon pepper
½ cup water
3 tablespoons red wine vinegar
Minced parsley for garnish

In 4-quart saucepan over high heat, heat unpeeled potatoes and enough water to cover to boiling. Reduce heat to low. Cover and simmer 20 to 30 minutes until potatoes are fork-tender. Drain, peel, and dice potatoes.

In 10-inch skillet over medium heat, melt butter and add onion. Cook until tender, about 5 minutes. Stir in sugar, salt, flour, and pepper until blended. Gradually stir in water and vinegar. Cook, stirring constantly, until mixture is slightly thickened and boiling. Gently stir in potatoes. Heat through. Garnish with parsley.

Serves 6

SPINACH

Black, white; up, down; spinach, ughhh . . .

Why does everybody grow up hating spinach and loving Popeye?

Spinach, properly cooked, tastes wonderful and is a tremendous source of iron.

Perhaps spinach's bad reputation came from the fact that it was always overcooked.

Perhaps spinach's bad reputation has come from the fact that until recently it was always overcooked and too salty and bitter and come to think of it, ughhh.

But now we know better about this leafy-green vegetable. We know we can eat it raw in a salad with warm oil dressing, chopped eggs, and croutons; we know we can bake it into casseroles and soufflés. And we know that steamed lightly, it's an absolute tastė treat.

Try these recipes and see if you can't put "spinach, ugghhh" into the lexicon of the past.

SPINACH PASTRIES

2 cans refrigerated crescent roll dough
1½ cups chopped, cooked spinach
1 cup grated Cheddar cheese
Salt and pepper
2 scallions, chopped
1 egg

Follow package directions and roll out dough.

Combine well-drained spinach, cheese, scallions, salt and pepper, and egg. Mix well.

Place 2 or 3 tablespoons of filling mixture in center of triangle and close dough around center securely. Place on cookie sheets. Bake 10 minutes longer than roll packages direct, or until well browned on top. Remove from oven, cut into sections, and serve hot.

Serves 10 to 12

SPINACH SOUP

2 lb. spinach
2½ quarts water
2 tablespoons oil
4 potatoes, peeled and diced
2 teaspoons salt
½ teaspoon pepper
2½ teaspoons lemon juice

Combine water, oil, and potatoes in a large kettle. Cook over medium heat 30 minutes. Remove from heat.

Remove potatoes and mash as fine as possible. Return mashed potatoes to liquid. Add salt and pepper and cook over low heat for 30 minutes.

Wash spinach, remove tough ribs, and shred or chop leaves fine. Add to potato mixture and cook over medium heat for 15 minutes, stirring occasionally. Add lemon juice and more salt and pepper to taste. Serve hot or cold.

Serves 6 to 8

SPINACH AND YOGURT SALAD

1 medium onion, thinly sliced
1 clove garlic, minced
2 10-oz. bags spinach
2 cups plain yogurt
½ cup chopped walnuts
2 tablespoons salad oil
2 tablespoons lemon juice
2 teaspoons crumbled dried mint
or
2 tablespoons chopped fresh mint
1½ teaspoons salt
½ teaspoon pepper

In covered 4-quart saucepan cook onion and garlic in ¼ inch boiling water over medium heat, until onion is tender, about 3 minutes. Remove cover; increase heat to high. Gradually add spinach to saucepan. Cook, stirring frequently, until spinach is just wilted. Drain and cool.

In large bowl, combine spinach mixture, yogurt and remaining ingredients. Toss gently until spinach is well coated. Cover and refrigerate at least 3 hours.

Serves 4 as a main dish or 6 as a side dish

HOT SPINACH SALAD

3 lb. spinach
1 teaspoon salt
¼ cup olive oil
2 cloves garlic, minced
3 tablespoons sliced almonds or pine nuts
¼ cup sliced green olives
¼ cup sliced black olives
1 tablespoon capers
2 tablespoons raisins

Wash and drain spinach. Sprinkle with the salt. Cook 5 minutes, then drain and chop.

Heat the oil in a skillet. Stir in the garlic and nuts until golden. Add the olives, capers, and raisins, mixing until coated. Mix in the spinach. Heat and serve.

Serves 4 to 6

CREAMED SPINACH

2 lb. fresh spinach
3 oz. sweet butter
2 tablespoons minced celery
¼ teaspoon tarragon or chervil
½ teaspoon sugar
½ cup cream
1 egg yolk
Salt and pepper
1 tablespoon dry cooking sherry

Clean and drain spinach; remove stems and chop leaves. Place in skillet with melted butter. Cook until moisture evaporates and spinach is cooked; this will take only a few minutes. Stir frequently. Add all other ingredients except sherry and season to taste. Do not boil after addition of cream. Simmer gently for 5 to 10 minutes. Add 1 tablespoon dry sherry during final cooking moments.

Serves 4 to 6

SQUASH

Some things just don't sound as good as they are. Squash is one of them.

One of the best things about squash, other than its absolutely delicious taste, is that it's available in one form or another all year long: Those that are harvested and cooked in the immature state are called summer squash and include Straightneck, Yellow, and maybe the king of squashes, Zucchini. The major winter squashes—Hubbard, Buttercup, and Gold Nugget are firm, fine-flavored, store very well, and are excellent for baking and pies. The best of the fall varieties are Royal Acorn, Table Queen, and Waltham Butternut. All in all, you will always find your produce section stocked with a variety of squash, and lots of them will not only be appealing to the palate, but because of their

If you let squash get too large and ripe, it gets . . . squashy.

sculptured shapes and extraordinary coloring, pleasing to the eye as well.

All squash should be picked when young and tender because if you let it get too large and ripe, it gets—well, squashy.

I'm going to give you a good mixture of squash recipes, and recommend that an excellent way to better health is to play a game of squash and then come home and eat some. I'm including pumpkin recipes in this section, too. Pumpkin can be a treat even if it's not Hallowe'en.

ACORN SQUASH WITH FRUITED RICE

3 medium acorn squash, cut in halves crosswise, seeded
6 tablespoons butter
⅓ cup brown sugar, packed
1½ teaspoons salt
¼ teaspoon powdered cloves
½ cup bourbon
¼ cup chopped onion
1 cup converted rice
2¼ cups water
1 medium apple, pared and chopped
⅓ cup chopped soft dried apricots
½ cup coarsely chopped pecans

Place squash, cut-side down, in 13 × 9-inch baking pan and pour ½ inch water into pan. Cover with foil and bake at 400° for 30 minutes. Remove from oven and turn squash cut side up.

Melt 4 tablespoons of butter and combine with brown sugar, ½ teaspoon salt, cloves, and ¼ cup bourbon. Spoon mixture evenly into squash. Cover with foil and continue to bake at 400° until squash is tender, about 30 minutes.

While squash is baking, sauté onion in remaining 2 tablespoons butter in 10-inch skillet until tender. Add rice. Cook and stir over low heat until rice is golden, about 3 minutes. Add water and remaining ¼ cup bourbon and 1 teaspoon salt. Bring to boil. Cover tightly and simmer 20 minutes. Remove from heat. Add apple, apricots, and pecans. Let stand, covered, until all liquid is absorbed about 5 minutes. Mound 1 cup rice mixture into each squash half.

Serves 6

BAKED BUTTERNUT SQUASH

1 large butternut squash, cut into pieces
¼ teaspoon cinnamon
¼ teaspoon nutmeg
½ cup brown sugar, packed
½ cup butter or margarine, melted
2 teaspoons lemon juice

Pare squash, remove seeds and fibers, and cut into 1-inch cubes. Place squash in 2-quart casserole or baking dish. Sprinkle with cinnamon, nutmeg, and brown sugar. Drizzle with melted butter and lemon juice. Bake, uncovered, at 375° for 45 minutes or until tender.

Serves 4

HONEYED BANANA SQUASH

2 lb. banana squash
Boiling water
½ cup honey
1 teaspoon salt
1 teaspoon cinnamon
3 tablespoons butter or margarine

Peel squash and cut into 2-inch squares. Arrange in a deep baking dish. Add enough water to barely cover squash. Also add honey, salt, cinnamon, and butter cut into small pieces. Cover tightly and bake at 375° for 2 hours or until squash is very tender.

Check occasionally and if liquid evaporates, add more boiling water, though liquid should have cooked away by the time the squash is done.

Serves 6 to 8

SUMMER SQUASH AND ZUCCHINI SAUTÉ

3 small summer squash
3 small zucchini
2 scallions
2 tablespoons butter
1 tablespoon oil
½ teaspoon sugar
Salt and pepper

Wash squash and zucchini, trim off ends, and cut them diagonally into ¼-inch slices as uniformly as possible. Chop scallions, including some of the green tops.

In a large skillet, heat butter and oil (oil keeps butter from burning). Add zucchini and squash slices. Then cook and stir them for 3 or 4 minutes. Stir in scallions and sauté mixture 2 or 3 minutes more, adding a dollop more butter if necessary. Don't overcook—the squash should retain some crispness. Season with sugar, salt, and pepper.

Serves 6

ZUCCHINI-PEPPER PIE

1 9-inch pastry pie shell, unbaked
3 medium zucchini (1 lb.), sliced thin
2 green onions with tops, sliced
1 large clove garlic, minced (optional)
2 tablespoons oil
1 medium tomato, peeled and chopped
1 medium green pepper, chopped
¾ teaspoon salt
½ teaspoon basil
¼ teaspoon pepper
3 eggs
½ cup heavy cream
¼ cup grated Parmesan cheese

Prick bottom of pie shell and bake at 450° for 8 minutes or until lightly browned. Cool.

Sauté zucchini, onions, and garlic in oil about 5 minutes, stirring occasionally. Stir in tomato, green pepper, salt, basil, and pepper. Cook over low heat, stirring occasionally, until vegetables are tender and liquid has evaporated, about 10 minutes.

Spread vegetables evenly in shell. Beat eggs and cream until mixed; pour over vegetables. Sprinkle with Parmesan cheese. Bake in preheated 350° oven for 30 minutes or until set.

Serves 6

ZUCCHINI CUTLETS

2 large zucchini
2 eggs, beaten
2 rounded tablespoons grated Romano cheese
Parsley
3 tablespoons cooking oil
1¼ cups seasoned bread crumbs
¼ teaspoon salt
Freshly ground pepper

Cut ends from zucchini, peel, and slice into strips approximately 1 to 1½ inches wide, 4 to 5 inches long, and ¾ inch thick.

Mix salt and pepper in with beaten egg. Heat cooking oil in large skillet until hot.

Mix cheese and bread crumbs. Dip slices of zucchini into egg, then into bread crumb mixture, and brown on all sides. Turn gently to avoid breaking slices. Add more cooking oil if necessary.

Remove to heated platter and sprinkle with parsley. Serve as is as side dish.

Serves 6

MARINATED ZUCCHINI

1 cup chili sauce
2 teaspoons grated Parmesan cheese
2 tablespoons olive oil
Salt, pepper
Pinch oregano
¼ teaspoon minced garlic
Juice of ½ lemon
4 large zucchini

Combine chili sauce, cheese, oil, salt and pepper to taste, oregano, garlic, and lemon juice and beat with whisk.

Wash and slice zucchini about ⅛-inch thick. Add to dressing and chill, turning several times, about 4 hours or longer.

Serves 6 to 8

ZUCCHINI FRITTERS

1½ lb. zucchini, cut in ¼-inch slices
6 green onions, finely chopped
6 sprigs parsley, finely chopped
¼ cup grated Romano or Parmesan cheese
1 clove garlic, minced
Salt
Freshly ground pepper
2 slices bread, made into crumbs
4 eggs
Olive oil

Boil zucchini 10 to 15 minutes. Drain.

Mix zucchini, onions, parsley, cheese, garlic, salt and pepper to taste, bread crumbs, and eggs.

Heat ½-inch olive oil in skillet. Drop zucchini mixture by large spoonfuls into oil and cook until browned on each side. Drain.

Makes 6 to 8 fritters

PUMPKIN SPICE CAKE

2½ cups sifted flour
1 teaspoon baking powder
1 teaspoon soda
1 teaspoon salt
¾ teaspoon cinnamon
¾ teaspoon cloves
1 cup granulated sugar
½ cup brown sugar, packed
¾ cup softened shortening
½ cup buttermilk
1½ cups cooked or canned pumpkin
3 eggs
Heavy cream, whipped
Cinnamon Glaze

Sift together flour, baking powder, soda, salt, cinnamon, cloves, and granulated sugar. Add brown sugar and shortening, buttermilk and pumpkin, and beat for 2 minutes. Add eggs and beat 2 minutes longer. Turn batter into 2 greased and floured 8-inch cake pans and bake at 350° for 30 to 35 minutes. Cool. Spread at least ½ cup whipped cream over one layer, top with another layer. Drizzle Cinnamon glaze over top and garnish with additional whipped cream.

Serves 6 to 8

CINNAMON GLAZE

2 cups sifted confectioner's sugar
1 teaspoon cinnamon
4 to 5 tablespoons hot whipping cream

Blend sugar, cinnamon, and hot cream until smooth. Drizzle over cake.

PUMPKIN PIE

2 eggs, lightly beaten
1½ cups canned pumpkin
¾ cup sugar
½ teaspoon salt
1 teaspoon cinnamon
½ teaspoon ginger
¼ teaspoon cloves
1⅔ cups evaporated milk or light cream
1 9-inch unbaked pastry shell

Combine eggs, pumpkin, sugar, salt, cinnamon, ginger, cloves, and evaporated milk. Turn into pastry shell. Bake at 425° for 15 minutes. Reduce temperature to 350° and bake 45 minutes longer or until knife inserted near the center of pie comes out clean.

Serves 6

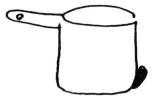

SWEET POTATOES (YAMS)

First things first: What's the difference between sweet potatoes and yams? The true yam, a tuberous root of African origin, weighs about seven pounds and resembles a semideflated football and is a different plant from the yellow sweet potato with fawn-colored skin and the dark, moist variety with reddish skin which we call yams even though they're not.

The main thing is it doesn't matter whether you use yams or sweet potatoes in recipes that call for one or the other—they are absolutely interchangeable—and what's more, they're also interchangeable with pumpkin and winter squash.

In recipes, yams, sweet potatoes, pumpkins, and winter squash are interchangeable.

FROM A TO Z

By any name, sweet potatoes or yams are scrumptious eaten merely baked or boiled with butter and any number of spices such as cinnamon, nutmeg, or ginger. They are also indescribably delicious mashed with pineapple, apples, or any other fruit.

Sweet potatoes are high in vitamin A, and can be eaten cold as well as hot, but to me, Mr. Mother Earth, the best bonus is that you can stick a sweet potato in a glass of water and watch it grow into a beautiful, dark-green vining houseplant.

There are lots of recipes for sweet potatoes or yams, but I'll only give you two or three because in the long run you'll dig 'em best just the way they're dug up.

SWEET POTATO PIE

3 eggs, slightly beaten
1 cup brown sugar, packed
1 cup milk
1 teaspoon cinnamon
½ teaspoon nutmeg
½ teaspoon ginger
½ teaspoon salt
¼ cup lemon juice
2 tablespoons melted butter or margarine
1½ cups cooked, pureed sweet potatoes
½ cup chopped pecans
1 9-inch pie shell (unbaked)

Combine eggs, sugar, milk, cinnamon, nutmeg, ginger, and salt and mix well. Add lemon juice and butter and blend.

Blend in sweet potatoes with rotary or electric mixer. Add pecans and mix well.

Pour mixture into pastry shell and bake at 375° for 50 to 60 minutes or until knife inserted near center of pie comes out clean.

Serve with whipped cream, if desired.

Serves 6

SWEET POTATO SALAD

1 to 1½ lb. sweet potatoes
Boiling water
1 cup thinly sliced celery
½ cup thinly sliced green onion
1 large red apple, diced
½ cup mayonnaise
1 teaspoon prepared mustard
½ teaspoon grated orange peel
1 tablespoon orange juice
2 tablespoons finely chopped, crystallized ginger
Salt and pepper
Crisp greens

Cook the sweet potatoes in boiling water to cover until tender when pierced, about 30 minutes. Drain. When cool enough to handle, peel the potatoes and then cut into ½-inch cubes. Combine the sweet potatoes, celery, onion, and apple.

In a small bowl stir together the mayonnaise, mustard, orange peel and juice, and the ginger. Pour the dressing over the potato mixture and mix well. Season to taste with salt and pepper.

Cover and chill at least 2 hours or as long as overnight.

To serve, line a shallow salad bowl with crisp greens. Pile sweet potato mixture on top.

Serves 4 to 6

SWEET POTATO CASSEROLE

8 medium sweet potatoes
¾ cup brown sugar or honey
¼ cup orange juice
Grated rind of 1 orange and 1 lemon
¼ teaspoon powdered cloves
¼ teaspoon cinnamon
¼ cup bourbon or brandy
½ cup diced dried apricots
4 tablespoons butter
Dash mace

Boil potatoes until tender. Pare and halve. Place in greased baking dish.

Heat together sugar, juice, rind, spices, and 3 tablespoons butter. Pour over sweet potatoes. Add other ingredients.

Bake at 350° for about 1 hour. Serve hot as side dish or cold as dessert.

Serves 10

YAM PUFFS

4 cups mashed cooked sweet potatoes or yams (use fresh baked potatoes only)
2 egg yolks
1 teaspoon salt
2 tablespoons brown sugar
¾ cup melted butter or margarine
½ cup flour
1 cup finely chopped nuts

Combine mashed sweet potatoes with egg yolks, salt, sugar, and ¼ cup of melted butter. Stir in flour and mix thoroughly. Form into bite-size balls. Dip in remaining melted butter and roll in nuts.

Place on baking sheet and freeze. When ready to serve, bake at 350° for 30 minutes, or until golden and hot throughout.

Makes about 4 to 5 dozen

TOMATOES

"I say tomato, you say . . ."

Thus has the tomato been immortalized in song!

And well it should be, for the gorgeous, rich-red, round, and firm tomato—which it should be when you buy it—is truly one of the most easy-to-get-along-with of all Nature's creations.

If there were such a thing as a Vegetable High School Graduating Class, Tomatoes would win "Best All Around" in a cakewalk:

Tomatoes make a sensational soup, hot or cold; are as necessary as lettuce to a salad. There is *no* sandwich which isn't better for joining forces with a tomato; you can use tomatoes with eggs; you can stuff them hot or cold with almost anything, you can eat them raw with absolutely no seasoning—and best of all, they have practically no

Tomatoes are the most easy-to-get-along-with.

calories. When it comes to versatility in vegetable-land, there's only one thing a tomato can't do: Be a Vegetable.

That's right. Tomatoes are botanically classified as Fruit.

I said tomatoes are best all-around. I never said they were perfect.

SWISS TOMATOES

6 medium tomatoes
Salt and pepper
2 cups grated Swiss cheese
1 egg, beaten
¼ teaspoon curry powder
3 tablespoons fine dry bread crumbs
2 tablespoons melted butter or margarine

Slice top from tomatoes, scoop out insides, and set the pulp aside. Sprinkle inside of tomato with salt and pepper. Mix tomato pulp, cheese, egg, and curry. Use mixture to stuff tomatoes.

Place in a shallow baking pan. Mix crumbs and butter and sprinkle over tops of tomatoes. Bake at 400° for 20 minutes or until tomatoes are soft but still hold their shape.

Serves 6

FRESH TOMATO SOUP

½ cup butter or margarine
2 tablespoons oil
2 medium onions, thinly sliced
2 tablespoons fresh thyme, minced (or 1 teaspoon dried)
1 tablespoon fresh basil, minced (or ½ teaspoon dried)
Salt and pepper
6 large tomatoes, peeled, cored, seeded, and chopped
¼ cup flour
3½ cups vegetable broth
1 cup heavy cream
Sugar

In a large heavy pot, heat ¼ cup butter and oil. Add onion, thyme, basil, salt and pepper to taste. Cook over medium heat until onions are soft. Add tomatoes and simmer until soft, about 10 minutes.

Blend flour with small amount of broth and stir into tomato mixture. Add remaining broth and simmer 5 minutes, stirring constantly.

Put soup through blender and blend until smooth. Return to heat and add cream and sugar to taste. Simmer, stirring constantly, until heated through, about 5 minutes. Add remaining butter and blend in.

Garnish with croutons.

Serves 8

BROILED TOMATOES

4 to 6 firm ripe tomatoes, unpeeled
2 tablespoons vegetable oil
1 or 2 cloves garlic, minced
¼ cup minced parsley
Salt
1¼ cup fine dry bread crumbs
Butter or margarine

Wash tomatoes and cut in half through stems. Saute gently, cut sides down, in the oil in skillet until some of the juice cooks out and tomatoes are tender. Turn and sauté, skin sides down, 1 minute.

Remove to shallow broiler-proof dish and keep warm. In remaining juice in skillet, cook garlic and parsley gently 2 to 3 minutes. Add salt to taste and the crumbs.

Sprinkle tomatoes lightly with salt and pile crumb mixture on top. Dot with butter and broil quickly until crumbs are browned.

Serves 4 to 6

ITALIAN TOMATO-CELERY CASSEROLE

1 1 lb. 13 oz. can tomatoes
2 teaspoons minced onion
1 teaspoon salt
⅛ teaspoon pepper
½ bay leaf
¼ teaspoon oregano
⅛ teaspoon whole basil leaves
¼ teaspoon Worcestershire sauce
Few drops Tabasco sauce
3 cups ½-inch toasted bread cubes
1 cup sliced celery
1 tablespoon cornstarch
1 tablespoon water
2 tablespoons soft butter or margarine

Drain liquid from tomatoes into a saucepan. Simmer for 5 minutes. Add onion and seasonings.

Layer 1 cup bread cubes, ½ cup celery, and half the drained tomatoes in a greased 1½-quart casserole. Repeat layers.

Remove bay leaf from tomato liquid. Combine cornstarch and water. Stir into hot liquid and simmer until thick, stirring constantly. Pour over casserole. Cover closely and refrigerate.

When mealtime approaches, scatter remaining 1 cup toasted bread cubes over top of casserole. Dot with butter or margarine. Bake at 350° for 30 minutes.

Serves 8

ITALIAN TOMATO SALAD

4 large tomatoes, sliced
4 red onions, sliced
¾ cup olive oil
¼ cup wine vinegar
2 tablespoons capers
2 teaspoons basil
1 teaspoon salt
¼ teaspoon pepper
Parsley sprigs

Alternate tomato and onion slices in overlapping circles on a platter.

Blend oil, vinegar, capers, basil, salt and pepper. Pour about half the dressing over tomatoes and onions. Cover with plastic wrap and chill thoroughly.

Decorate platter with parsley sprigs and serve with remaining caper dressing.

Serves 6 to 8

COLD TOMATOES STUFFED WITH EGGPLANT

2 large tomatoes
6 tablespoons olive oil
1 large onion, chopped
1 clove garlic, chopped
1 stalk celery, chopped
1 medium eggplant
2 tablespoons tomato paste
3 tablespoons wine vinegar
½ teaspoon sugar
Salt and pepper

Cut off ½-inch slice from stem ends of tomatoes. Scoop out pulp with teaspoon. Chop pulp coarsely and set aside.

Turn tomato shells upside down on plate or rack and refrigerate until ready to fill.

Put about half the oil in large frying pan and sauté onion, garlic, and celery until golden (about 5 minutes). Cut eggplant (no need to peel it) into ½-inch cubes. Add to vegetables in skillet. Cook over medium heat for 15 minutes, stirring often. (During this cooking, add remainder of oil as needed.)

Stir in reserved tomato pulp, tomato paste, vinegar, sugar, salt and pepper to taste. Cook 10 minutes longer. Put mixture into covered container, cool, and refrigerate for at least 12 hours.

At serving time fill each tomato shell with eggplant salad.

Leftover salad keeps in the refrigerator for days, and makes a great appetizer or cold vegetable dish.

Serves 2

MIXED VEGETABLES

I suppose when most people think of "mixed vegetables" the first thing that comes to mind is succotash.

No wonder so few people bother to think about mixed vegetables. (Although the succotash recipe which follows is really rather good.)

In truth, mixing vegetables is about as easy and rewarding as mixing paint—anything will go with anything else—almost.

There are, however, a few basic dishes, or methods of cooking your crazy, mixed-up veggies, that are important to know. Those are included in the following pages.

Any other combinations or methods of cooking vegetables I'll leave to you.

It's real easy. You can't possibly get mixed up.

VEGETABLE TEMPURA

Tempura batter
¼ cup flour
1 large sweet potato
1 small acorn squash
1 large green pepper
1 large yellow onion
6 large mushrooms
2 large carrots
Vegetable oil

Prepare tempura batter and chill for at least 2 hours.

Pare sweet potato and cut into ¼-inch slices; halve acorn squash, seed; cut into ¼-inch strips and pare; halve and seed pepper; cut into 1-inch pieces; cut onion into ¼-inch slices and separate into rings; cut mushrooms into ¼-inch slices; pare carrots and cut into ¼-inch diagonal slices.

Pour vegetable oil into a 10-inch skillet to a depth of 3 inches. Heat until a dab of batter dropped into the oil crisps and browns quickly. Fry no more than 6 to 8 pieces at a time in the hot oil until food rises to the surface; turn and fry until golden, about 1 minute. Remove with skimmer or slotted spoon to a cookie sheet lined with paper toweling. Keep hot in oven preheated to 250°.

Skim the surface of the oil to remove any excess pieces of batter; check temperature; fry remaining food, about 6 pieces at a time.

Give each diner an individual bowl of dipping sauce. Serve tempura hot, either on individual plates or on a platter.

TEMPURA BATTER

1 egg yolk
1 cup ice water
¾ cup sifted flour

Combine egg yolk and ice water in a large bowl; sift in flour and mix lightly. Batter should have a consistency of pancake batter, thin enough to run off a spoon easily. Chill at least 2 hours; if too thick, thin with a few drops of cold water.

DIPPING SAUCE

⅓ cup Japanese soy sauce
⅓ cup mirin (sweet sake) or sweet white wine
1 cup water

Combine soy sauce, mirin or sweet wine, and water in a 2-cup measure. Pour into 4 individual dipping bowls.

Serves 4

SUCCOTASH

2 cups shelled lima beans (about 2 lb.)
½ cup water
1 teaspoon salt
1 teaspoon sugar
¼ teaspoon pepper
3 tablespoons butter or margarine
2 cups fresh corn kernels cut off the cob (about 6 ears)
¼ cup light cream

Place lima beans, water, salt, sugar, and pepper in a large saucepan; cover and cook over moderately low heat until beans are almost tender, about 20 to 25 minutes. Add butter and corn and cook uncovered about 5 minutes, or until corn is tender and all the water is absorbed. Add the light cream and heat until the mixture is completely warmed through.

Serves 6 to 8

VEGETABLE-NUT LOAF

⅓ cup butter or margarine
1 cup chopped mushrooms
2 large onions, finely chopped
¼ cup chopped green pepper
3 cups grated carrots
1½ cups chopped celery
½ cup sunflower seeds
¾ cup coarsely chopped walnuts
5 eggs, beaten
3 cups soft whole wheat bread crumbs
Basil
Oregano
Salt and pepper

Melt butter in skillet; add mushrooms, onions, and green pepper, and cook until tender but not browned. Combine mushroom mixture in bowl with carrots, celery, sunflower seeds, walnuts, eggs, bread crumbs, and basil, oregano, salt and pepper to taste.

Line bottom of 9 × 5-inch loaf pan with waxed paper; then grease paper and sides of pan generously. Turn mixture into pan and bake at 325° for 1 hour.

Note: The nut-loaf mixture can also be used to form little "meatballs" or shaped into hamburger-type patties to be fried or baked.

Serves 8

VEGETABLE SOUP

Kernels from 1 ear of corn
½ medium eggplant, cubed in 1-inch pieces
1 large pale-skinned potato, washed and cubed
1 large red bell pepper, seeded and cut in 1-inch pieces
2 medium zucchini, thickly sliced
1 yellow onion, peeled and cut in 1-inch squares
5 mushrooms, sliced
4 cloves garlic, peeled and thinly sliced
3 green onions, coarsely chopped
1 cup shredded cabbage
1 dill pickle, very thinly sliced
1½ cups chopped fresh spinach
2 tomatoes cut in thin wedges
Approx. 3 quarts water
Salt, pepper
2 tablespoons olive oil
2 tablespoons red wine vinegar
Ground cumin
Cayenne pepper
Oregano

To prepare the soup, just wash and trim the vegetables as required; chop or slice them and put them all together in a very large kettle with the water. Add salt and pepper, as well as the olive oil, vinegar, and spices to taste. Simmer the soup for at least ½ hour and serve piping hot with bread and cheese.

Serves 6 to 8

RATATOUILLE

¼ cup olive oil or vegetable oil
¼ cup (½ stick) butter
3 garlic cloves, minced
2 onions, sliced
1 eggplant, peeled and cubed
2 zucchini, washed and sliced
2 green peppers, seeds removed and cut in strips
¼ cup flour
4 large tomatoes, peeled and sliced
Salt, pepper
½ teaspoon sugar
2 teaspoons capers, drained
5 white bread slices, toasted and buttered, cut into triangles

In a large skillet heat oil and butter, add garlic and onions and sauté until translucent. Add eggplant, zucchini, and green pepper. Sprinkle with flour, combine well. Cover and cook slowly about ½ hour, stirring occasionally. Add the tomatoes and simmer uncovered until the mixture is thick. Season with salt and pepper to taste. Add sugar and capers during the last 15 minutes of cooking. Serve hot or cold with toast.

Serves 8

MIXED VEGETABLE CURRY

1 lb. small potatoes, peeled and cut in halves
1 lb. green beans, cut in 1-inch pieces
¾ lb. carrots, peeled, quartered lengthwise, and cut in 1-inch pieces
2 cups (or 1 9-oz. package frozen peas, thawed)
½ cup butter or margarine
1 tablespoon curry powder
1¼ teaspoons salt
⅛ teaspoon pepper
¼ cup plain yogurt
1 tablespoon tomato paste

In large covered saucepan cook potatoes, green beans, and carrots together in boiling salted water to cover until vegetables are barely tender, about 15 minutes. Add peas. Continue cooking until vegetables are just tender, about 5 minutes. Drain. While vegetables are cooking, melt butter in a large skillet. Add curry powder, salt, and pepper. Sauté until curry turns slightly darker, about 30 seconds. Add vegetables. Stir to coat well. Simmer until piping hot, about 5 minutes. Remove from heat. Combine yogurt and tomato paste. Stir into vegetables. Spoon onto a serving dish.

Serves 6 to 8; makes about 5 cups

MIXED VEGETABLE STIR-FRY

2 tablespoons oil
1 medium clove garlic, cut in half
2 carrots, cut diagonally in ¼-inch slices
2 ribs celery, cut diagonally in ¼-inch slices
3 or 4 green onions with tops, cut in 1-inch pieces
2 medium yellow summer squashes, cut diagonally in ¼-inch slices
1 green or red pepper, seeded and cut in ½-inch strips
1 tablespoon soy sauce
Salt and pepper to taste
1 tablespoon sliced almonds (optional)

In heavy skillet, heat oil and garlic over medium-high heat until garlic is golden brown; discard garlic. Add carrots and celery, stir-fry 3 to 4 minutes or until partially cooked. Add onions, squashes, and green pepper, stir-fry 2 to 4 minutes or until vegetables are still crisp-tender. Sprinkle with soy sauce, salt, pepper, and almonds.

Serves 4 to 6

There is nothing quite so sad as a soggy salad.

Salads

Even someone who's never seen a kitchen knows how to make a salad, right?

Wrong, wrong, wrong!

Oh, if we're talking lettuce and tomatoes on a dish covered with some store-bought dressing, okay, I guess that's a salad.

But wouldn't you rather eat a *salad?*

I mean, there are so many wondrous combinations of fruits and vegetables, of hot and cold, of this dressing or that . . .

We'll get to the recipes in a minute. Right after a couple of important tips: Buy only the freshest, crispest vegetables for salads (or for anything, for that matter); wilted lettuce that isn't supposed to be wilted is a definite salad-making no-no; be sure to serve your cold salads *cold*—after you've washed your ingredients and *drained them thoroughly* so the water won't freeze up on the lettuce and ruin it, put the salad in the refrigerator. Do not pour your dressing onto the salad until just before you serve, as there is nothing quite so sad as a soggy salad. And think carefully about the dressing—obviously fruit salads will taste better with one dressing, whereas vegetable salads will be better with another. Salads are a good dish with which to experiment with dashes of herbs and spices here and there. You'll be surprised that once you get the hang of it, you can invent salads which will literally be full, delicious meals.

Before we bound to the table, however, a word about Lettuce and other nonspendable Green Stuff.

There are many, many different kinds of lettuce available almost everywhere at any time of the year—varieties and prices vary, depending on the season.

Since lettuce is at least as important to the taste of a salad as dressing, but since the entire subject of Which-Lettuce-Tastes-Best is purely subjective—one person's Romaine might be someone else's Ptomaine—let your palate be your guide.

Try everything—Butter lettuce, Boston lettuce, Romaine, Bibb, and of course the "Philodendron" of lettuce, Iceberg. Each has a slightly different taste and texture from the other. You might settle on one particular favorite, or two or three, or you might even find you like to mix several different lettuces in your green salads. Just be sure that whichever lettuce you choose is brightly colored, fresh, and clean of brown-tipped or mottled leaves.

And as long as you're tasting lettuce, start nibbling bits and pieces of the other greens: Watercress, Endive, Dandelion Greens—the list of potential salad ingredients is almost endless. I just came back from the local produce mart and they were selling—ready?—pressed Fiddlehead Ferns for salad greens! I'm sure they were good, but Mr. Mother Earth couldn't bear to eat a Fern. I'd feel like a cannibal.

Lettuce now try these salad recipes on for size.

CAESAR SALAD

1 large head romaine
1 egg
4 tablespoons oil
2 tablespoons red wine vinegar
2 cloves garlic, mashed
Few drops Worcestershire sauce
¼ Teaspoon dry mustard
Peppercorns
2 slices toast, cut in cubes
3 tablespoons lemon juice
¼ cup Parmesan cheese
Anchovies, for garnish (optional)

Wash romaine and dry.

Set egg in hot water to warm, but not congeal. Mix oil and vinegar. Add garlic and egg. Then add Worcestershire sauce and dry mustard. Pour dressing over lettuce. Grate fresh pepper over salad.

Add toast cubes. Pour on lemon juice. Sprinkle with Parmesan cheese. Garnish with anchovies if you wish.

Serves 4

GREEK SALAD

1 head Boston lettuce or romaine, torn into bite-size pieces
2 ripe tomatoes, cut into wedges
8 black olives (preferably Kalamatas from Greece)
½ small Bermuda onion, peeled and sliced into rings
½ cup crumbled Feta cheese
Dressing

Arrange all the salad ingredients in a bowl and at serving time toss gently with dressing.

Serves 4 to 6

DRESSING

⅓ cup olive oil
2 tablespoons fresh lemon juice
Salt, pepper
½ teaspoon sugar
¼ teaspoon oregano

Shake together dressing ingredients.

SPANISH RICE SALAD

2 cups cold cooked rice
½ cup cooked, chilled, thinly sliced carrots
½ cup cooked, chilled cauliflowerets
¼ cup oil
1 tablespoon lemon juice
1 teaspoon onion juice
2 teaspoons wine vinegar
1 teaspoon celery seed
1 teaspoon dry mustard
Salt and pepper
2 tablespoons chopped pimento or ripe olives

Combine rice, carrots, and cauliflower. Combine oil, lemon juice, onion juice, vinegar, celery seed, dry mustard, salt and pepper to taste. Add just enough dressing to moisten salad. Garnish with pimento or olives

Serves 6

FARMER'S CHOP SUEY

1 large cucumber
1 medium green pepper
1 cup sliced radishes
6 green onions, sliced
3 tomatoes
¼ teaspoon salt
Dash pepper
1 cup cottage cheese
1½ cups sour cream
1 teaspoon lemon juice

Peel and cube cucumber. Remove seeds and membrane from green pepper and cut the flesh in chunks. Combine cucumber, green pepper, radishes, and onions. Mix well and chill.

Just before serving, core tomatoes, cut in large cubes, and toss gently with the chilled vegetable mixture.

Combine salt, pepper, cottage cheese, sour cream, and lemon juice and mix well.

Add dressing to salad and toss lightly. Garnish with additional tomato wedges and radish roses. Serve at once.

Serves 6

VEG-MAC SALAD

2 quarts water
1 teaspoon garlic salt
1 teaspoon salt
2 cups macaroni
¼ cup lemon juice
2 tablespoons oil
1 cup sliced celery
½ cup chopped green onions
1½ to 2 teaspoons salt
½ teaspoon coarse pepper
½ cup sour cream
¼ cup mayonnaise
Lettuce

Combine water, salt, and garlic salt and bring to a boil. Gradually add macaroni and cook, 10 to 15 minutes until tender. Drain and rinse macaroni with cold water. Drain well.

Stir in lemon juice and oil and chill at least 1 hour. Add celery, onion, salt, pepper, sour cream, and mayonnaise and mix thoroughly.

Line salad bowl with lettuce and arrange salad on lettuce. If desired, garnish with green pepper rings, tomato wedges, or parsley.

Serves 6 to 8

SURFER SALAD

1 medium pineapple
1 medium orange, peeled
1 cup thinly sliced carrots
1 cup thinly sliced cucumber
¼ cup oil
¼ cup orange juice
2 tablespoons white wine vinegar
1 tablespoon honey
1 teaspoon lemon juice
2 teaspoons fresh mint

Cut pineapple in half lengthwise through crown, leaving shells intact. Refrigerate one-half for later use. Remove fruit from remaining half. Core and dice fruit. Slice orange into cartwheels.

Combine pineapple, orange, carrots, and cucumbers in bowl.

Combine oil, orange juice, vinegar, honey, lemon juice, and mint in screw-top jar. Shake well. Pour over pineapple mixture. Toss several times. Spoon fruit into pineapple shell.

Serves 4

Dressings and Sauces

When I was a very, very young person, I used to tell a "joke" that I'm sure was in your repertoire, too:

"What did the Mayonnaise say to the Lettuce?"

"What?"

"Close your eyes—I'm dressing."

I don't know if my sense of humor has advanced much, but I know that my appreciation of mayonnaise as a dressing for salads has declined.

Don't misunderstand. I *love* mayonnaise—I'll spread mayonnaise on practically anything between two pieces of bread and even use it occasionally as the main ingredient of a salad dressing.

But, as the Lettuce joke is merely the tip of the Iceberg—ohhh, groan . . . so Mayonnaise is merely the tip of the Dressings.

For lots of good tips on dressings and sauces, please turn the page.

ROQUEFORT DRESSING

2 oz. Roquefort cheese
2 tablespoons boiling water
½ teaspoon onion juice
½ teaspoon garlic juice
¼ teaspoon Worcestershire sauce
Dash hot pepper sauce
1 cup mayonnaise
½ cup buttermilk
¼ teaspoon salt

Crumble cheese and dissolve in boiling water and set aside for 30 minutes. Beat mixture with rotary beater until smooth. Add onion and garlic juices, Worcestershire and pepper sauces, mayonnaise, buttermilk, and salt, then blend well. Let stand 24 hours.

Makes 2 cups

FRENCH DRESSING

¼ cup white or red wine vinegar
¾ cup salad oil
2 tablespoons water
¼ teaspoon paprika
1 teaspoon sugar
Salt

Combine vinegar, oil, water, paprika, sugar, and salt to taste in a jar or bottle with a tight lid. Cap and shake thoroughly before using.

Makes 1 cup.

Variations: With white wine vinegar, crush a few sprigs of fresh dill, rosemary, or French tarragon. Add longer sprigs to container and allow to season before using.

With red wine vinegar, add a sprig of oregano or marjoram or a clove of garlic. Allow to season before using.

POPPY SEED DRESSING

¾ cup oil
¼ cup wine vinegar
1 tablespoon lemon juice
2 tablespoons minced onion
1 tablespoon catsup
½ teaspoon dry mustard
½ teaspoon salt
1 tablespoon sugar
2 dashes cayenne
1 cup mayonnaise
2 tablespoons poppy seeds

Place oil, vinegar, lemon juice, onion, catsup, mustard, salt, sugar, and cayenne in a bowl. Beat at medium speed 3 minutes. Add mayonnaise and beat 3 minutes longer. Add poppy seeds and beat until blended.

Makes about 2 cups

HERB BUTTERMILK DRESSING

1 cup buttermilk
2 teaspoons chives, minced
1 teaspoon chervil, minced
1 teaspoon watercress, finely chopped
1 teaspoon tarragon, minced
¼ teaspoon dry mustard
1 teaspoon sugar
Salt

Mix buttermilk, chives, chervil, watercress, tarragon, mustard, sugar, and salt to taste. Blend thoroughly and chill for at least 1 hour.

Makes 1 cup

CREAMY ITALIAN DRESSING

¾ cup mayonnaise
1 tablespoon wine vinegar
1 tablespoon lemon juice
1 tablespoon salad oil
1 tablespoon water
1 teaspoon Worcestershire sauce
½ teaspoon oregano
1 teaspoon sugar
1 small garlic clove, minced

Combine mayonnaise, vinegar, lemon juice, salad oil, water, and Worcestershire sauce. Blend well. Mix in oregano, sugar, and garlic. Chill.

Makes 1 cup

THOUSAND ISLAND DRESSING

1 cup mayonnaise
½ teaspoon salt
¼ teaspoon pepper
Dash cayenne
1 tablespoon lemon juice
1 tablespoon catsup
1 teaspoon Worcestershire sauce
2 tablespoons pickle relish
2 tablespoons minced parsley
⅓ cup diced celery
1½ tablespoons diced pimento
1 tablespoon minced onion

Combine mayonnaise, salt, pepper, cayenne, lemon juice, catsup, and Worcestershire sauce. Beat together until well blended. Add pickle relish, parsley, celery, pimento, and onion and stir until well mixed. Chill several hours.

Makes 1½ cups

CITRUS FRENCH DRESSING

¼ cup olive oil
1 tablespoon grapefruit juice
1 tablespoon orange juice
1 tablespoon lemon juice
2 tablespoons honey
1 teaspoon salt
¼ teaspoon paprika
Dash cayenne

Combine oil, grapefruit, orange and lemon juices, honey, salt, paprika, and cayenne in small jar and shake until thoroughly blended.

Makes about ½ cup

WHITE SAUCE

2 tablespoons butter
2 tablespoons flour
1 cup milk
Salt, pepper

Melt butter in a saucepan and stir in flour, mixing thoroughly for a few minutes. Then pour in milk, beat with a whisk over medium heat 2 minutes, until thickened, and season to taste with salt and pepper.

A thicker sauce can be made by adding an additional tablespoon each of butter and flour.

Makes about 1 cup

CHEESE SAUCE

Make white sauce as above. Add up to one cup grated Cheddar or Swiss cheese. To spice it up, add ½ teaspoon dry mustard, a dash of paprika, and a little Worcestershire sauce.

FLUFFY HONEY DRESSING

2 eggs
½ cup honey
¼ cup lemon juice
2 tablespoons frozen orange juice concentrate, thawed
⅛ teaspoon salt
½ cup heavy cream, whipped
2 teaspoons grated lemon peel

Beat eggs in a small saucepan and stir in honey, lemon juice, orange juice concentrate, and salt. Cook and stir over low heat until thickened. Cool and fold in whipped cream and peel. Serve with fruit salad.

Makes 2 cups

BLENDER HOLLANDAISE SAUCE

3 egg yolks
2 tablespoons lemon juice
¼ teaspoon salt
Pinch of white pepper
1 stick (4 oz.) butter, heated to bubbling in a small pan.

Place egg yolks, lemon juice, salt, and pepper in jar of blender. Cover, and blend at high speed for 30 seconds. Uncover and, still blending at high speed, start pouring in the hot butter by droplets. The heat of the butter warms the egg yolks, and by pouring very slowly you are giving the yolks time to absorb the butter. When about ⅔ of the butter has gone in, sauce should be a thick cream, and you can pour a little more quickly.

Makes ¾ cup, serving 4

Fruit

If there's one thing I believe nobody can live without, it's fruit. Whether eaten fresh or frozen, taken off the tree or plucked from the produce counter, baked into pies or cakes or churned into ice cream or sherbet, blended into drinks or preserved as jams and jellies, fruit is truly the spice of life. (Somehow that feels like a mixed metaphor, but when I get to talking about fruit, I go bananas. . . .)

I am not alone in my love for this family of succulent comestibles. The joys of fruit have been known through all the ages. "A day without orange juice is a day without sunshine" . . . "An apple a day keeps the doctor away . . ."

Since most fruit is best eaten in its natural form—a raw pear or a bowl of berries or a bunch of grapes can provide the ultimate in taste and nutrition—I am not going to include very many recipes for cooked fruit in this book. Actually, almost any fruit can be baked into a pie or boiled and eaten hot, but there are certain little extra things you might want to know about the individual fruits that are readily available, and a few rather interesting and off-beat recipes you might want to try.

The joys of fruit have been hailed through the ages.

So let's run through the various fruits, give you just a smidgen of information on each, and then when you're ready to go fruit, we'll toss in some recipes.

APPLES A fitting beginning to our odyssey through fruits. After all, wasn't an apple the beginning of everything? Apples, which come in tart or sweet green, and soft or firm red and yellow, are full of mineral salts, vitamins C and B, and fructose, the best natural sweetener under the sun. Apples can be used in anything from salads to curries to crepes, and provide quick energy when eaten raw. Also make excellent targets for budding archers.

APRICOTS Fresh or dried, apricots—or *A*-pricots—are absolutely delicious, besides providing lots of vitamins and minerals. This is one fruit I personally like only two ways: Raw, a bit on the soft side, because they're sweeter that way, or baked into a pie or Danish Pastry. Oh, Apricot Jam is pretty good and there's an Apricot Chutney that's out of the world . . . but enough of this chitchat about Apricots, it's time to go:

Wasn't an apple the beginning of everything?

FRUITS

BANANAS Although I don't want to get into a debate over Darwin vs. Creation, I must admit I have an uncommon craving for bananas and it would be no surprise to find an ape in my family tree. I always keep at least four or five bananas in the kitchen, the riper the better, for snacking, mixing with blender drinks, or sometimes combining with peanut butter when a real case of the munchies comes on. One of the best things about bananas is that they're cheap—or, in today's lexicon, "affordable," since nothing is "cheap" anymore. Whether you like them fried, sautéed, or deep-fried and plunged into icy water the Chinese way, take this part-monkey banana-junkie's word: This succulent fruit will go with practically any edible you can think of, so you can count on banana recipes to have appeal.

I must admit I have an uncommon craving for bananas.

Which do you prefer: ☐ *Sex* ☐ *Night baseball* ☐ *Ripe cherries*

BERRIES Many years ago, if something was really wonderful, people would say: "It's the berries!" Well, I still say it—when it comes to fruit, there's almost nothing more wonderful than a berry—whether it be straw, rasp, boysen, goose, or my personal favorite, blue. (Although I adore berries right off the vine or with a bit of cream and sugar, blueberries baked into cupcakes or pancakes or blintzes or waffles absolutely drive me wild! In fact, I might even make a Swedish movie someday called *Wild Blueberries.*) I have found that berries bought fresh frozen, without the addition of sugary syrup, can be delicious, especially if eaten just before they're completely thawed. During fall and winter berries can be very, very expensive, so best to buy frozen or to freeze some yourself when they're in season.

CHERRIES Which do you prefer—sex, night baseball, or red, ripe, juicy cherries? For me, it's a toss-up. No, it's not. I confess. I'll take the cherries. Like George Washington, I cannot tell a lie. But I could *never* chop down a cherry tree!

Citrus: The richest source of vitamin C.

CITRUS FRUITS Oranges, lemons, limes, grapefruit . . . all delicious and by far the richest natural source of vitamin C. Citrus should really be eaten only raw and cold, or squeezed into the world's most popular juices, although some people like to warm up half a grapefruit and cover it with honey. As far as I'm concerned, there's no way a wedge of ice-cold citrus fruit can be a lemon, even if it is.

GRAPES Grapes come in many sizes and colors, although almost all are about the size of large marbles and are either green or purplish. Some grapes have seeds and some do not; you'll simply have to discover which are which through trial and error—although eating a grape with seeds can hardly be called an error. Make grapes into juice, jam, jelly, a necklace, even . . . they're marvelous. Beulah, peel me a grape!

MANGO This tropical, exotic fruit is very expensive, but you're worth it, so when mangoes are in season pick up a couple. Then, besides eating it raw (make sure the fruit is very soft for maximum sweetness), you might want to try the sherbet recipe you'll find in this section. It's a sure-bet to please you.

MELONS Probably the favorite crop of outdoor gardeners in warm climates (and almost sinfully expensive to buy in colder spots during the winter), there are Cranshaw melons, and watermelons, and Persian Melons and cantaloupe melons and honeydew melons and millions of melons . . . . Naturally the best way to eat a melon is fresh alone or mixed with other fresh fruits, but I think maybe you'll take to the cold soup recipe I've included here.

PEACHES What comes immediately to mind as the ultimate in soft,

Peaches are best when just a tad overripe.

delicate, after-dinner taste treats? Peaches and Cream. Peach Melba . . . Of course, like all the rest of the fruit family, I like my peaches raw—(with the fuzz rubbed off if there's a bit too much)—and preferably room temperature as opposed to cold. But you might like to try a recipe or two baking with peaches or using them as part of a blender drink. Either way, everything will be peachy, you can be sure.

PEARS In looking for interesting tidbits about pears, I discovered that history's premiere pear-lover was Pliny, who mentions 33 varieties! Well, I've only been lucky enough to stumble over four or five, but whether they be green or yellow or reddish, firm or soft, sweet or tart—pears are truly the glory that was Rome.

PINEAPPLE Did you know that Pineapples are members of the Bromeliad family—the same family that produces the Aechmea Fasciata, that greyish-green plant with the long pink-and-blue-tipped flower you see in the flower shops? Well, they are. And besides being sweet and juicy served fresh, ice-cold, they are also reproducers—you can twist the top off a pineapple, let roots form in water or perlite, then pot in planting mix and watch it grow, including, eventually, a new tiny pineapple!

RHUBARB A friend of mine told me he once came home and his wife served him up a rhubarb pie. "How come it's two feet long?" he asked. "Because," she replied, "I couldn't find any shorter rhubarb!" Anyway, Rhubarb is a fruit, and a rather tasty one when baked, so with a warning that it has a high oxalic acid content and should not be eaten more than once a month, have a whack at a rhubarb pie—and don't forget to cut up the fruit so you don't get into a rhubarb with an irate spouse.

Okay. It's time to go fruit! Now try these recipes and then please stick around, because when we get finished with the fruit, we're going to go Nuts!

DANIELLE'S PEACH COBBLER

1 stick butter
1 can (# 2½) sliced peaches
1½ cups sugar
1 cup self-rising flour
½ cup milk

Melt butter in oblong pan (9 × 13 × 2 inches) in oven.

Mix peaches and syrup in saucepan and bring to boil. Mix sugar, flour, and milk to make batter. Pour batter into pan in melted butter. Add hot peaches over batter and bake at 350° for 25 minutes or until golden brown.

Serve hot with softened vanilla ice cream or whipped cream.

Serves 4 to 6

STRAWBERRIES WITH GRAND MARNIER SAUCE

3 to 4 pints strawberries, rinsed and hulled
2 tablespoons sugar
3 egg yolks
⅓ cup sugar
¼ cup Grand Marnier (or other orange-flavored liqueur)
1 cup heavy cream

Toss strawberries with sugar and chill.

In top of a double boiler over barely simmering water, whisk egg yolks and sugar until thick and pale, about 5 to 6 minutes. Place pan in a shallow bowl of ice water.

When cool, place a piece of plastic wrap directly on surface and chill. An hour before serving, whisk Grand Marnier into sauce. Whip cream until it holds soft peaks. Fold into sauce. Chill.

Serve berries in dessert dishes and pass the sauce.

Serves 6 to 8

STRAWBERRY CHEESE PIE

1 8-oz. package cream cheese
3 tablespoons half and half
1 9-inch baked pie shell
1 quart strawberries, washed and stemmed
2 tablespoons cornstarch
Pineapple juice
¾ cup sugar

Blend cheese and half-and-half and spread on cooled pie shell. Chill.

Slice half of the largest berries and set aside. Mash remaining berries and put in blender. Add cornstarch and mix to make paste. Add enough pineapple juice to make 1½ cups liquid. Add sugar and then cook until thick and transparent, stirring constantly. Cool.

Pour half of mixture into pie shell and arrange sliced berries over top. Pour on remaining mixture. Chill. Serve with whipped cream, if desired.

Serves 6

CELESTIAL STRAWBERRIES

2 1-pint baskets strawberries
½ cup red currant jelly
2 tablespoons orange-flavored liqueur
Whipped cream (optional)

Rinse and hull berries. Dry on paper towels. Put 1 cup in blender, the rest in bowl. Cover and chill bowl.

Set jelly and liqueur in small pan over low heat until melted. Pour into blender over strawberries. Blend until smooth. Chill.

Shortly before serving, place whole berries in glass serving bowl and pour sauce over them. Mix gently.

Pass whipped cream separately if desired.

Serves 4

STUFFED PEACHES

6 fresh peaches
3 oz. crushed hard macaroons
1 egg yolk
1½ oz. sugar
1 oz. butter

Slice the peaches in half and remove the pits. Take out a little flesh from the center and mix with crushed macaroons, egg yolk, sugar, and butter. Blend and spoon the mixture into the peaches.

Bake in a buttered ovenproof dish at 375° for about 25 minutes.

Serves 6

POACHED PEARS WITH STRAWBERRY SAUCE

6 firm, barely ripe pears with stems
½ cup sugar
1 tablespoon lemon juice
1 cinnamon stick
4 or 5 cloves
1½ cups frozen unsweetened strawberries, slightly thawed
Grated rind and juice of ½ orange

In a pan large enough to hold the pears, combine the sugar, lemon juice, cinnamon, and cloves. Add 3 cups water and simmer for 5 minutes.

Peel the pears; also core. Cut a thin slice from the bottom of each one so it will stand upright.

Place pears in simmering syrup, cover and poach until tender when pierced with a toothpick, 20 to 25 minutes. (Don't overcook or they'll be mushy.) Let pears cool, then refrigerate overnight in syrup.

Just before serving, puree strawberries in blender with orange rind and juice. Add additional sugar to taste.

Drain pears. Serve on dessert plates and pour strawberry sauce over each.

Serves 6

ORANGE-GLAZED PEAR NUT BREAD

1 16-oz. can pear halves
1½ cups all-purpose flour
¾ cup granulated sugar
1 tablespoon baking powder
1 teaspoon salt
¼ teaspoon allspice
1 cup whole wheat flour
¼ cup oil
1 egg, beaten
1 tablespoon grated orange peel
1 cup chopped walnuts
2 to 3 tablespoons orange juice
1 cup powdered sugar

Drain pears, reserving syrup. Reserve 1 pear half for garnish. Puree remaining pears.

Add reserved syrup to pureed pears to measure 1 cup. Sift together all-purpose flour, granulated sugar, baking powder, salt, and allspice. Stir in whole wheat flour.

Mix pureed pears with oil, egg, and orange peel. Stir into flour mixture. Blend in nuts. Pour into a greased 9 × 5-inch loaf pan. Cut reserved pear half into 6 slices. Place slices on batter. Bake at 350° for 50 to 55 minutes.

Blend orange juice into powdered sugar to make thin glaze. Remove warm bread from pan and spoon glaze over top. Store bread overnight before slicing.

MANGO SHERBET

1 cup water
½ cup sugar
Dash salt
2 mangoes, peeled and sliced
½ cup light cream
¼ cup lemon juice
2 egg whites

In saucepan, combine water, ¼ cup sugar, and salt. Cook 5 minutes. Cool.

In blender, puree mango with cream. Stir in cooled syrup and lemon juice. Freeze in one 6-cup or two 3-cup refrigerator trays until partially frozen.

Beat egg whites to soft peaks. Gradually add ¼ cup sugar, beating to stiff peaks. Turn frozen mixture into chilled mixer bowl, break into chunks. Beat smooth. Fold in beaten egg whites. Return to cold tray. Freeze firm. Garnish each serving with fresh mint, if desired.

Serves 6 to 8

SUNSHINE TART

¾ cup whole wheat flour
¾ cup flour
¼ teaspoon salt
¾ teaspoon grated orange peel
¾ cup shortening
3 tablespoons orange juice
1 8-oz. and 1 3-oz. package cream cheese, softened
3 bananas
3 tablespoons whipping cream
¾ cup orange marmalade
1 tablespoon orange-flavored liqueur

Mix flours, salt, and ½ teaspoon orange peel. Cut in shortening. Add orange juice and toss with fork to form dough. Press in bottom and up sides of a 9-inch tart pan with removable bottom. Pierce with fork. Bake at 425° for 12 to 15 minutes.

Beat cream cheese. Mash 1 banana and add with cream to cream cheese. Stir in remaining orange peel. Spread over cooled tart shell. Chill until firm, at least 3 hours. Slice remaining 2 bananas and arrange overlapping slices around tart. Heat marmalade until melted and bubbly. Stir in liqueur. Brush glaze over top of tart. Chill 15 minutes before serving.

Serves 6

FRUIT SOUP

2 tablespoons Minute quick-cooking tapioca
Pinch salt
2 tablespoons honey
2¼ cups orange juice
1 apple
1 banana
½ small pink grapefruit
2 peaches
1 pint strawberries

Mix tapioca, salt, honey, and 1¼ cups orange juice well. Let stand 5 minutes. Bring to a boil over medium heat, stirring often. Cool for 20 minutes. Add ½ to 1 cup more orange juice, depending on consistency you want.

Cut up fruits and add to soup. Chill.

Serves 4 to 6

APPLE PIE

8 tart apples
¾ cup sugar
2 tablespoons flour
½ teaspoon nutmeg
½ teaspoon salt
Pastry for 2-crust 9-inch pie
1 tablespoon lemon juice
1 tablespoon butter

Peel and slice apples thin. Combine sugar, flour, nutmeg, and salt, blending well. Add sugar mixture to apples and mix well.

Roll out ⅔ dough and fit into 9-inch pie plate. Turn apples into pastry-lined pie plate and sprinkle with lemon juice and dot with butter. Flute the edges of lower pie crust and weave remaining pastry rolled out and cut into strips over filling to form lattice.

Bake at 425° for 45 to 50 minutes.

APPLESAUCE

1⅓ lb. tart apples
½ cup water
Dash salt
½ to 1 cup sugar
1 teaspoon cinnamon

Peel, core, and cut apples into eighths to make 4 cups. Bring water to a boil and add salt. Add apples. Simmer until apples are soft but not mushy. Add water as needed to prevent burning. Add sugar to taste and cinnamon. Strain sauce if necessary.

Serves about 6

STUFFED BAKED APPLES

6 large baking apples
½ cup firmly packed brown sugar
½ cup golden raisins
½ teaspoon cinnamon
¾ cup honey
½ cup water
1 tablespoon butter or margarine
1 teaspoon grated lemon rind

Wash apples and core, then pare about ⅓ of the way down from stem end. Stand in a 13 × 9 × 2-inch baking dish.

Mix brown sugar, raisins, and cinnamon in a small bowl. Spoon into center of apples, packing down well.

Combine honey, water, butter or margarine, and lemon rind in a small saucepan. Heat, stirring constantly, to boiling. Pour over apples. Cover.

Bake at 350°, basting often with syrup in dish, for 1 hour or until apples are tender but still firm enough to hold their shape.

Cool in dish on a wire rack, spooning syrup over apples often to make a rich glaze.

Serves 6

APPLE CAKE

2 cups unsifted all-purpose flour
2 cups granulated sugar
2 teaspoons baking soda
1 teaspoon cinnamon
½ teaspoon nutmeg
½ teaspoon salt
4 cups finely diced, peeled raw apple (about 1½ lb.)
½ cup chopped walnuts
½ cup soft butter or margarine
2 eggs
Confectioner's sugar

Into large bowl, sift flour with granulated sugar, soda, cinnamon, nutmeg, and salt.

Add apple, nuts, butter, and eggs. Beat until just combined—it will be thick. Turn into greased 13 × 9 × 2-inch baking pan.

Bake at 325° for 1 hour, or until top springs back when lightly pressed with fingertip. Cool slightly in pan on wire rack. Sprinkle with confectioner's sugar.

Serve warm, cut into squares. Top with whipped cream or ice cream if desired.

Serves 8

BANANA NUT LOAF

¾ cup sugar
½ cup oil
2 eggs
1 cup mashed bananas
1¾ cup sifted flour
2 teaspoons baking powder
½ teaspoon baking soda
½ teaspoon salt
¼ cup chopped nuts

Combine flour, baking powder, baking soda, salt. Combine sugar and eggs and beat until frothy. Add mashed bananas and nuts. Add flour mixture and blend. Place in greased 5 × 9-inch loaf pan. Bake at 325° for 1 hour.

Nuts

Nuts come in all manner of shapes and sizes and flavor.

Your basic list of these wondrous little goodies which you can purchase raw or cooked, in the shell or shelled, in jars plain or salted, includes peanuts, cashews, walnuts, filberts, almonds, pecans, chestnuts, and, of course, me.

Nuts have myriad uses in vegetable cookery. They marry perfectly with many salads, they're a terrific addition to stews and casseroles, dinners go from soup to nuts, and certain recipes even go from nuts to soup.

Here are a few nutty recipes.

Peanuts, walnuts, filberts, almonds, pecans, chestnuts, and me.

PECAN PIE

3 eggs
⅔ cup sugar
½ teaspoon salt
⅓ cup butter, melted
1 cup light or dark Karo syrup
1 cup pecan halves
1 9-inch unbaked pie crust

Beat eggs, sugar, salt, butter, and corn syrup together with rotary beater. Mix in pecan halves. Pour into 9-inch pastry-lined pie tin. Bake at 400° for 40 to 50 minutes or until set and pastry is nicely browned. Cool.

Serve cool or slightly warm.

PEANUT PANCAKES

2 cups pancake mix or buttermilk biscuit mix
1 cup crushed unsalted peanuts
½ teaspoon cinnamon
2 tablespoons brown sugar
Whipped cream, vanilla yogurt, jelly, or fruit-flavored syrup

Prepare pancake batter according to package directions. Add peanuts, cinnamon, and brown sugar. Mix lightly and let stand 10 minutes. For each pancake, spoon 2 tablespoons batter onto a hot, lightly greased griddle. Bake until browned on one side, turn and cook on other side.

Serve in stacks topped with whipped cream, yogurt, jelly, or syrup and an additional sprinkling of crushed peanuts, if desired.

Makes about 28

PEANUT BUTTER SOUP

2 tablespoons butter or margarine
2 tablespoons grated onion
½ cup thinly sliced celery
2 tablespoons flour
3 cups vegetable broth
½ cup smooth peanut butter
¼ teaspoon salt
2 teaspoons lemon juice
2 tablespoons roasted peanuts

Melt butter in a saucepan over low heat. Add onion and celery. Sauté about 5 minutes. Add flour and mix until well blended. Stir in chicken broth and allow it to simmer about 30 minutes. Remove from heat and strain broth. Stir in the peanut butter, salt, and lemon juice until well mixed.

Serve hot in cups. Garnish each cup with a teaspoon of chopped peanuts.

Serves 6

ALMOND SOUP

1 cup blanched almonds, toasted
¼ cup butter or margarine
¼ teaspoon salt
Dash freshly ground pepper
1 tablespoon cornstarch
1 cup water
1 egg, well beaten
1 cup half and half
Toasted sliced almonds

Grind almonds ½ cup at a time in blender. Heat butter until lightly browned. Add ground almonds, salt, and pepper. Blend cornstarch with water and add to almond mixture. Simmer 10 minutes, stirring frequently. Beat egg with half and half. Slowly stir in broth mixture. Heat, stirring constantly. Do not boil.

Serve hot or well chilled. Garnish with toasted sliced almonds.

Serves 6 to 8

PEANUT BUTTER FUDGE

1 cup dry milk powder
1 cup peanut butter
1 cup honey
½ teaspoon vanilla
3 tablespoons wheat germ
Chopped nuts

Mix all ingredients together, except nuts. Shape into rolls or logs. Roll in nuts. Keep in refrigerator and cut just before serving.

Makes 12 pieces

Pasta

The pasta family doesn't have a Godfather, but it does include spaghetti, spaghettini, linguine, noodles, fettucine, macaroni, ad infinitum.

Pasta should be boiled with a little salt added to the water and removed just before it becomes soft.

The only thing easier than making your own pasta is buying it, which frankly, I recommend you do.

Pasta dishes are endless, but usually it's the sauce that makes the meal. Pasta tastes good with practically anything—cheese sauces, butter sauces, vegetable sauces, tomato sauces, and so forth.

Here are some general pasta recipes—and one general pasta tip: Be sure not to overcook, because overcooked pasta will inevitably became paste, and I have no recipes for that.

Pasta dishes are endless.

SOUR CREAM PASTA SAUCE

1 12-oz. package spinach noodles
2 tablespoons butter or margarine
2 tablespoons olive oil
2 cloves garlic, cut in halves
½ cup white wine
1½ cups sour cream
1 cup chopped walnuts
½ cup finely chopped parsley
2 tablespoons basil
½ teaspoon salt

Prepare spinach noodles according to package directions. Heat butter and olive oil in skillet until hot. Cook and stir garlic in butter and oil until garlic is brown. Remove garlic and discard. Stir wine into butter and oil. Simmer, uncovered, stirring occasionally, until half of wine has evaporated. Mix in sour cream, walnuts, parsley, basil, and salt. Cook and stir over medium heat until hot. Serve immediately over hot cooked spinach noodles.

Serves 6

FETTUCINE A LA PERRY STREET

8 oz. fettucine
¼ cup butter or margarine
1 cup grated Parmesan cheese
¾ cup slivered almonds, roasted
½ cup whipping cream, whipped
2 tablespoons sliced green onions
Salt and pepper
Minced parsley

Cook noodles in boiling salted water in large saucepan as package directs. Turn into colander to drain. In same pan, melt butter and stir in drained noodles. Heat and gently stir-toss 1 to 2 minutes. Add cheese, almonds, whipped cream, onions, salt, and pepper to taste. Toss lightly to mix. Sprinkle with parsley and additional almonds and cheese if desired. Serve at once.

Serves 3 as main dish, or 6 to 8 as first course

SPAGHETTINI AL PESTO

1⅔ cups fresh basil leaves, packed closely
¼ cup parsley sprigs
2 cloves garlic, chopped
⅓ cup pine nuts
½ cup freshly grated Parmesan cheese
½ teaspoon salt
½ cup olive oil
1 pound spaghettini
3 tablespoons butter

In blender put basil, parsley, garlic, pine nuts, cheese, salt, and oil. Blend at high speed for a minute or two until mixture is reduced to a paste. Turn motor off once or twice and push pesto down from sides of blender jar with rubber spatula.

To serve: Cook spaghettini in lots of boiling salted water according to package directions. Drain and toss with butter until coated. Mix pesto sauce into piping hot spaghettini, tossing with two forks and serve on warm plates.

Serves 4

GREEN NOODLES WITH ALMOND BUTTER

½ cup butter or margarine
½ cup sliced blanched almonds
1 tablespoon lemon juice
8 oz. green noodles

Melt butter in heavy skillet, add almonds, and sauté until almonds are golden brown. Stir in lemon juice. Meanwhile cook noodles in boiling salted water until tender and drain in colander. Toss noodles with almond butter and serve at once.

Serves 4 to 6

MANICOTTI

12 manicotti shells
1 medium zucchini, diced
2 tablespoons butter
1½ cups cottage cheese
1½ cups shredded Cheddar cheese
1½ cups spaghetti sauce

Cook manicotti shells in 4 quarts boiling water about 10 minutes, or until almost tender. Drain and rinse in cold water.

In large skillet, cook zucchini and butter about 10 minutes, stirring occasionally. Stir in cottage cheese and 1 cup Cheddar cheese. Stuff manicotti with cheese mixture.

Arrange in single layer in shallow 2-quart baking dish. Spoon sauce over manicotti. Cover with foil and bake at 375° for 30 minutes. Uncover and sprinkle with remaining cheddar cheese. Bake 10 to 15 minutes longer, or until hot and bubbling.

Serves 6

MARINARA SAUCE

2 to 3 tablespoons olive oil
3 large cloves garlic
2 large cans Contadina Italian tomatoes
2 tablespoons tomato paste
1 teaspoon salt
½ teaspoon pepper
1 small dried red chili, crushed
1 tablespoon oregano, crushed
1 teaspoon sugar

Put olive oil into a heavy iron skillet. Chop up garlic and brown lightly. Then pour in tomatoes (chopped up first.) Add 2 tablespoons tomato paste and mix well to thicken. Add salt, pepper, chili, oregano, sugar, and mix well. Simmer on medium heat with no cover for 30 to 45 minutes. When the sauce has changed to a slightly orange color, turn heat down and cook 1 hour.

Serves 6

LASAGNA

1½ lb. spinach (2 cups chopped, packed spinach)
1 onion, chopped
1 to 2 tablespoons olive oil
2 cloves garlic, minced
2 lb. Ricotta cheese
¼ lb. grated Romano or Parmesan cheese
3 eggs, beaten
Salt, pepper
2 to 3 tablespoons chopped, fresh parsley
½ lb. Mozzarella cheese
1 lb. lasagna noodles
1½ quarts tomato or marinara sauce

Wash spinach, chop coarsely. Chop onion. Sauté with olive oil and minced garlic.

Combine Ricotta cheese, grated Romano cheese, spinach, beaten eggs, and chopped parsley. Mix well. Season with salt and pepper to taste.

Grate Mozzarella cheese coarsely.

Cook noodles with oil *al dente*. Drain, run cold water over them, and pat dry. Grease large pan. Arrange a layer of lasagna noodles on bottom, then mixture of Ricotta cheese and spinach. Then sprinkle Mozzarella cheese, then spoon some tomato sauce on. Begin again with a layer of noodles, Ricotta-cheese mixture, Mozzarella cheese, tomato sauce. Keep repeating until all is used up. Finish with sauce on top.

Cover baking pan tightly with aluminum foil. Bake at 350° for 40 minutes. Take off foil. Bake 10 to 15 minutes uncovered.

Serves 6 to 8

MACARONI FRUIT SALAD

2 cups macaroni
1 tablespoon salt
3 quarts boiling water
1 13¼-oz. can pineapple tidbits
1 11-oz. can mandarin oranges, drained
1 cup black grapes, halved and seeded
1 cup finely chopped celery
1 apple, diced and dipped in lemon juice
½ cup sour cream
½ cup mayonnaise
1 teaspoon lemon juice
Lettuce
½ cup chopped nuts

Slowly add macaroni and salt to boiling water. Cook, stirring occasionally, until tender. Drain, rinse with cold water, and drain again. Drain liquid from pineapple, reserving ¼ cup liquid. In a large bowl combine macaroni, pineapple, oranges, grapes, celery, and apple. In a small bowl, blend sour cream, mayonnaise, reserved pineapple juice, and lemon juice until smooth. Toss macaroni mixture with sour cream mixture. Chill well. Serve in lettuce-lined bowl. Sprinkle with nuts.

Serves 6 to 8

MACARONI AND CHEESE WITH CHILES

2 cups medium elbow macaroni
¼ cup butter or margarine
3 tablespoons flour
1 teaspoon salt
2 to 4 cloves garlic, minced
⅛ teaspoon pepper
3 cups milk
¼ cup grated onion
1 4-oz. can chopped green chiles
1 2-oz. jar pimento, chopped
3 cups shredded Jack cheese
½ cup crushed tortilla chips
Paprika

Cook macaroni until tender but firm; drain. Melt butter in large saucepan. Blend in flour and salt, garlic, and pepper. Cook, stirring constantly, 2 minutes. Slowly add milk, stirring until smooth. Add onion, chiles, and pimento. Cook until thickened. Stir in cheese, cook until melted.

Combine macaroni and cheese sauce. Pour into 2½-quart casserole. Top with tortilla crumbs and sprinkle with paprika. Bake at 350° for 25 minutes. Serve at once.

Serves 6

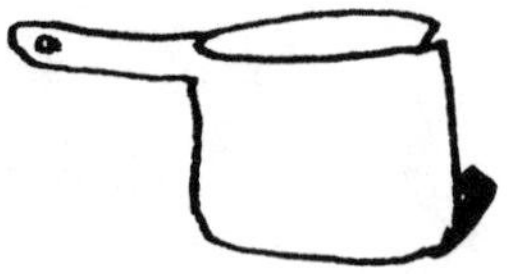

Blender Drinks

There is absolutely no way to succeed as a vegetable cooker without a blender. If you feel like taking a big plunge into more sophisticated cookery you can purchase an expensive food processor, some of which will do everything except actually serve the dish. But your ordinary blender will almost always fill the bill.

Blenders do just what they say they will do: Whip, stir, puree, aerate, crumb, chop, grind, mix, grate, pulverize, churn, liquefy—and, oh yes, blend.

Many recipes call for the use of a blender to change the texture of certain foods so that they will marry properly into the specific recipe. But the best use for the blender is to make drinks, especially for breakfast: Some carob milk, a couple of ripe bananas, a bit of sour cream, a tablespoonful of protein powder, a dash of cinnamon, a taste of nutmeg, and whatever else you feel like putting in will practically carry you through the day.

Although blender drinks are fun to invent yourself, here are some recipes to help you get the feel.

The best use for the blender is to make drinks, especially for breakfast.

COCONUT WHEAT GERM BREAKFAST

¼ cup coconut cream
1 cup nonfat milk
1 egg
2 tablespoons wheat germ
¼ cup frozen juice concentrate (orange or pineapple)

Combine coconut cream, nonfat milk, egg, wheat germ, and fruit juice in blender container. Blend until smooth. Pour into cold glass and serve immediately.

Serves 1

HAWAIIAN ENERGY DRINK

⅓ cup chopped pineapple
⅓ cup chopped guava
⅓ cup chopped papaya
½ cup plain yogurt
1 tablespoon nonfat dry milk
1½ tablespoons protein powder

Combine pineapple, guava, papaya, yogurt, dry milk, and protein powder in blender. Blend until smooth.

Serves 1

PEACH SPOON DRINK

1 egg
⅓ cup cold water
1 cup peeled and diced peaches
½ cup nonfat dry milk
1 cup crushed ice

Combine egg, water, peaches, and dry milk in blender. Blend 2 seconds. Add crushed ice and blend until smooth. Pour into tall 16-oz. glass. Serve with spoon.

Serves 1

HOT CAROB CEREAL DRINK

⅓ cup nonfat dry milk
1 cup granola cereal
1 tablespoon carob powder
¼ teaspoon vanilla
or
1 teaspoon instant coffee
1 cup hot water
1 tablespoon honey or sugar to taste

In blender combine dry milk, cereal, carob powder, and vanilla or coffee. Add hot water and honey and blend. Pour into cups. Top with whipped cream, sprinkled with granola, if desired.

Serves 2

Eggs

It has been said that eggs are the perfect food.

They certainly are delicious in many, many ways: Hard-cooked, boiled, scrambled, fried, baked, omelets, sauces, appetizers, salads—you name it.

Just be sure you don't eat too many eggs as they contain huge amounts of cholesterol which may bring on problems of the heart.

Probably the best use of eggs is in omelets, where it is possible to add any spice, fruit, or vegetable you desire.

The most important thing about making an omelet is to beat the eggs thoroughly with water and not milk. They should be cooked in a small amount of oil or butter in a covered skillet or omelet pan to make sure they are fluffy and lightly browned. Don't be afraid to season with anything that strikes your fancy and be sure to serve piping hot.

I can't stress enough the importance of keeping your egg intake down to an absolute minimum, but when you do feel it's time for an egg dish, allow me to egg you on with these recipes.

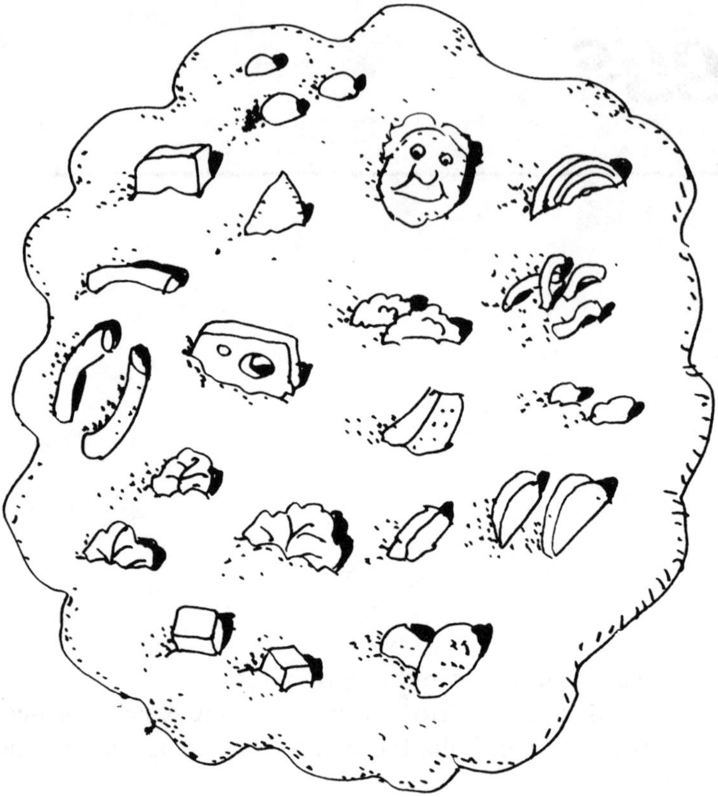

The best use of eggs is in omelets, where it is possible to add anything.

SPANISH-ONION OMELET

- 1 medium Spanish onion
- 5 tablespoons butter
- ¼ cup sour cream
- ½ teaspoon dill weed
- ¾ teaspoon salt
- ⅛ teaspoon pepper
- 6 eggs
- 2 tablespoons water
- 1 tomato, sliced
- Parsley sprigs

Peel and thinly slice onion. Separate into rings. Melt 4 tablespoons butter in skillet. Add onion rings and cook over low heat until tender. Stir in sour cream, dill, ¼ teaspoon salt, and pepper. Keep warm.

Beat eggs with water and remaining ½ teaspoon salt. Heat a 10 or 12-inch skillet. Add remaining 1 tablespoon butter, tilting pan to coat sides and bottom. When bubbling, add egg mixture. Cook until set on bottom, lifting sides to allow uncooked portion to run underneath. Spoon onions onto center of omelet. Fold one third of omelet over onions. Slide omelet onto platter, flipping to make another fold. Garnish with tomato slices and parsley sprigs.

Serves 3

CHUNKY EGG SALAD

12 hard-cooked eggs, quartered
¼ cup mayonnaise
¾ teaspoon salt
3 tablespoons milk
Dash pepper
2 stalks celery, sliced
½ cup sliced pimento-stuffed olives
2 teaspoons chopped onion
Lettuce leaves

In large bowl, combine mayonnaise, milk, salt, and pepper. Toss eggs gently with remaining ingredients except lettuce. Refrigerate.

To serve, place in lettuce-lined bowl or on lettuce-lined plates.

For egg salad spread for sandwiches, prepare recipe as above but finely chop eggs, celery, and olives.

Serves 6

CHERRY OMELET SUPREME

6 eggs, separated
¼ cup cream sherry
2 tablespoons sugar
1 tablespoon flour
¼ cup butter or margarine
Cherry Sauce

Beat egg yolks with sherry, sugar, and flour until well blended. Beat egg whites until stiff but not dry. Fold egg whites into yolk mixture until well blended. Heat butter in a large skillet. Pour egg mixture in and cook without stirring. When lightly browned on bottom, place skillet under broiler and cook until omelet is puffed and golden. Fold in half and slide onto warm serving plate. Spoon cherry sauce over omelet and serve at once.

Serves 3

CHERRY SAUCE

1 tablespoon cornstarch
¼ cup cream sherry
1 8-oz. can crushed pineapple
1 1-lb. can dark sweet pitted cherries, well drained

Combine cornstarch, sherry, pineapple, and cherries. Stir over low heat until sauce bubbles and thickens slightly.

Makes about 2½ cups

HUEVOS RANCHEROS

2 tablespoons oil
1 clove garlic, minced
1 small onion, chopped
½ teaspoon oregano
2 green chiles, mashed
1 1 lb. 12 oz.-can tomatoes, chopped
Salt
6 eggs
½ cup shredded cheese

Heat oil, add garlic and onion and cook until golden. Stir in oregano, chiles, and tomatoes. Simmer uncovered to thicken. Add salt to taste.

Break each egg into a saucer and slide into sauce. Simmer until eggs are set. Sprinkle with cheese and heat until melted. Serve on tortillas.

Serves 6

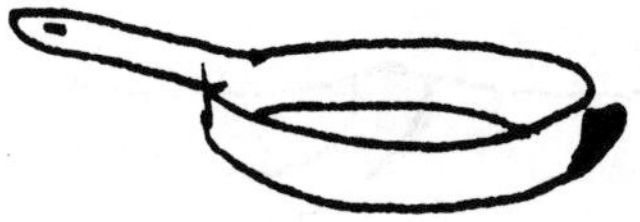

Cheese is the source of valuable amounts of protein.

Cheese

Cheese, when added to your vegetable diet, is a source of indescribable taste treats as well as vital amounts of protein.

Whether your dish contains Swiss cheese, Cheddar cheese, cottage cheese, or any of the dozens of natural cheeses—note I said *natural* as opposed to processed—it's bound to be better for the addition.

Raw or cooked in sandwiches, salads, soups, sauces, dips, appetizers, omelets, whatever—cheese is indispensable to a lacto-vegetable diet.

Is it any wonder you smile when you say cheese?

MOZZARELLA MARINARA

2 lb. Mozzarella cheese
2 eggs, beaten
1 cup flour
2 cups seasoned bread crumbs
2 tablespoons Parmesan cheese
Oil for frying
Marinara sauce

Cut cheese into ½-inch slices. Dip into beaten egg, then flour, and into egg again, then into seasoned bread crumbs mixed with Parmesan cheese.

Place breaded cheese in a single layer on a plate and chill at least 30 minutes.

Fry in ½ inch hot oil until browned on one side, turn and brown the other. Drain on absorbent paper.

When serving, spoon some marinara sauce onto plate, put a cheese slice in the sauce, then top with more sauce.

Serves 4

FOUR-CHEESE QUICHE

1 lb. Jack cheese
½ lb. sharp Cheddar cheese
½ lb. mild Cheddar cheese
½ lb. Mozzarella cheese
2 cups milk
3 eggs
¼ teaspoon cumin
2 9-inch pie crusts (unbaked)

Grate the cheeses and mix in a bowl. Beat eggs and add to milk. Add cumin. Mix well with the cheeses. Turn into the pie crusts and bake at 350° for 30 minutes or until knife inserted near center comes out clean. Let stand 5 minutes before serving.

This recipe can be expanded by adding 2 cups chopped "vegetable-of-choice."

Serves 6

WELSH RAREBIT

1 lb. aged Cheddar cheese, cubed
1½ cups milk
4 tablespoons butter
½ cup flour
2 tablespoons dry mustard
¾ cup beer
2 teaspoons Worcestershire sauce
2 teaspoons A-1 sauce
2 dashes Tabasco sauce
½ teaspoon cayenne
¼ teaspoon salt

Pour milk into double boiler and when warm add cheese, cut into small cubes, stirring until dissolved.

Melt butter and sift flour, mustard, cayenne, and salt into melted butter. Mix well until thick paste is formed and then add to milk and cheese, stirring constantly. Cook for 10 minutes, then add beer, Worcestershire sauce, A-1, and Tabasco. Keep warm until served. Serve over toast or English muffins.

Serves 8

INDIA SPREAD

1 8-oz. package cream cheese
½ cup crumbled Blue cheese
¼ cup finely cut dates
¼ cup finely chopped chutney
1 tablespoon lemon juice
¾ cup finely chopped pecans or walnuts

Beat cream cheese until fluffy. Add Blue cheese, dates, chutney, lemon juice, and mix thoroughly. Stir in ½ cup nuts. Put in serving dish. Sprinkle with remaining nuts and chill. Serve with crackers.

Makes about 2 cups

TANGY CHEESE SPREAD

½ lb. Cheddar cheese
2 tablespoons minced onion
2 tablespoons vinegar
1 clove garlic
1 teaspoon dry mustard
1 teaspoon Worcestershire sauce
2 tablespoons butter or margarine, softened
1 tablespoon chili sauce
⅛ teaspoon dill weed

Shred cheese. Rub mixing bowl with a cut clove of garlic. Add all ingredients and blend until smooth. Transfer to a covered container and store in refrigerator until ready to use.

Makes 2½ cups

CHEESE SOUP

2 tablespoons butter
1 clove garlic, minced
2 tablespoons flour
½ cup dry white wine
2½ cups milk
⅛ teaspoon pepper
⅛ teaspoon nutmeg
½ lb. Cheddar cheese, cubed
2 egg yolks
½ cup heavy cream
Grated Parmesan cheese

Melt the butter in a heavy saucepan. Add the garlic and cook, stirring so that it won't burn, until the butter is slightly flavored. Then discard the garlic. Stir in the flour to make a smooth paste.

Cook 2 to 3 minutes, stirring constantly. Add the wine, milk, seasonings, and cheese. Cook over moderate heat, stirring frequently, until the cheese has melted.

Beat the egg yolks and heavy cream together. Dribble a little of the hot mixture into the eggs, then combine the two, stirring constantly with a wooden spatula.

Heat to the boiling point but do not cook further. Serve at once with grated Parmesan.

Serves 6

RICOTTA PANCAKES

½ lb. Ricotta cheese
½ cup sifted flour
1 teaspoon baking powder
⅔ cup half and half
3 eggs, separated
1 tablespoon honey
½ teaspoon vanilla
½ teaspoon almond extract
Honey Sauce

Combine cheese, flour, and baking powder. Blend in half and half. Add egg yolks, honey, vanilla, and almond extract. Beat egg whites until stiff peaks form. Fold in beaten whites until blended. Cook on preheated griddle until undersides are browned. Turn and cook until other sides are browned. Serve with honey sauce.

Makes 12

HONEY SAUCE

½ cup butter or margarine, melted
½ cup honey
¼ cup Grand Marnier

Combine melted butter, honey, and Grand Marnier, blending thoroughly.

EXTRA CREAMY CHEESECAKE

1 lb. cream cheese
2⅔ cup plus 3 tablespoons sugar
Salt
3 eggs
½ teaspoon almond extract
1 cup dairy sour cream
1 teaspoon vanilla extract
Toasted slivered almonds (optional)

Beat cheese until fluffy. Gradually beat in ⅔ cup sugar and a dash of salt. Add eggs one at a time, beating well after each addition. Beat until smooth. Add almond flavoring and pour into buttered 9-inch pie pan. Bake at 350° for 25 minutes.

Remove from oven and let cool away from drafts for 20 minutes. While cake is cooling, beat sour cream, 3 tablespoons sugar, a dash of salt, and the vanilla together. Pour over top of cake. Return to oven, bake 10 minutes longer. Sprinkle with almonds, if desired. Cool and serve.

Serves 7 or 8

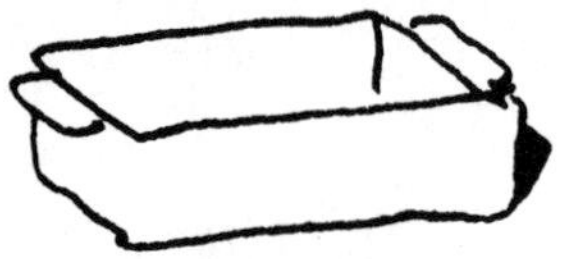

Rice

When you talk of staples, rice is almost always at or near the top of the list.

Besides the most common usage for rice—throwing it at weddings—rice is used, always boiled not-too-hard and not-too-soft (like pasta—*al dente)* as a bed for steamed or stir-fried vegetables, alone as a side dish such as pilaf, and even as dessert in puddings and cakes.

I prefer brown rice, but if you prefer the white, go ahead and use it in spite of the fact it has virtually no nutritional value compared to the brown.

Just to show you that rice truly can be a grain alone as opposed to an ingredient, here are some of my favorite recipes.

White rice has virtually no nutritional value compared to the brown.

BROWN RICE BURGERS

1 large onion, finely chopped
3 cloves garlic, minced
1 cup finely chopped water chestnuts
½ cup diced green pepper
Oil
½ cup minced parsley
4 cups cooked brown rice
2 cups shredded carrots
2 large eggs, beaten
1 cup whole wheat flour
Salt and pepper

Sauté onion, garlic, water chestnuts, and green pepper in 3 tablespoons oil for 10 minutes. Mix with parsley, rice, carrots, eggs, and flour. Add salt and pepper to taste. Drop mixture in ¼-cup quantities onto oiled, hot griddle. Brown on both sides.

Serve with toppings, such as tomatoes, lettuce.

Serves 8

RICE PUDDING

2½ cups cooked brown or white rice
½ cup raisins
½ teaspoon grated lemon rind
1 teaspoon lemon juice
½ cup honey
½ teaspoon vanilla
3 eggs
2½ cups milk

Place rice, raisins, rind, and juice in a buttered 1½-quart baking dish. Beat together remaining ingredients and pour over rice and raisins. Stir to mix. Bake 30 minutes or until pudding is set.

Serves 4

HONEY RICE

3 cups cooked rice
½ cup seedless raisins
2½ cups milk
½ cup honey
2 tablespoons butter or margarine
1 teaspoon grated lemon peel
1 tablespoon lemon juice

Combine rice, raisins, milk, honey, and butter. Bring to a boil, reduce heat, and simmer for 15 minutes, stirring occasionally. Stir in lemon peel and juice.

Serves 6

LEMON PILAF

1 cup sliced celery
1 cup chopped green onions with tops
2 tablespoons butter or margarine
3 cups cooked rice
1 tablespoon grated lemon rind
1 teaspoon salt
¼ teaspoon pepper

Sauté celery and onions in butter until tender. Add rice, lemon rind, and seasonings; toss lightly. Continue cooking over how heat about 2 minutes or until thoroughly heated, stirring occasionally. Serve with your choice of condiments, such as raisins, chutney, sliced almonds, toasted coconut.

Serves 6

RICE AU GRATIN

3 cups hot cooked rice
1½ cups grated Cheddar cheese
3 tablespoons butter or margarine
½ teaspoon curry powder
2 slices bread, crumbled or cubed

Toss rice with 1 cup cheese. Spoon into buttered baking dish; top with remaining cheese. Bake at 350° for 10 to 15 minutes or until cheese melts. Meanwhile, melt butter; stir in curry. Add bread crumbs and brown lightly. Remove rice from oven; sprinkle with curried crumbs.

Serves 6

RICE, CHEESE, AND OLIVES

½ cup rice
2 cups water
1 cup milk
½ lb. shredded sharp Cheddar cheese
1 egg, beaten
¼ teaspoon salt
Pepper
⅓ to ½ cup sliced stuffed olives
6 tablespoons buttered bread crumbs

Boil rice with water in small saucepan, simmer until tender-firm. Heat milk over low heat. Stir in cheese, egg, salt, and pepper to taste. Fold in drained rice. Place half of rice mixture in bottom of buttered small casserole (about 1 quart). Sprinkle with half of sliced olives. Add remaining rice to form another layer and sprinkle with remaining olives. Cover with buttered bread crumbs. Bake at 350° for 55 minutes.

Serves 4

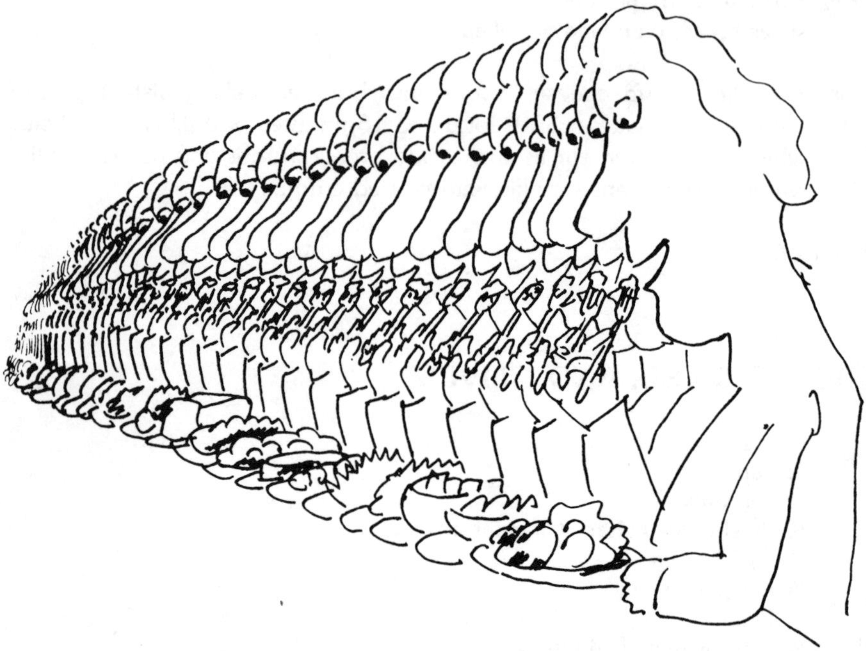

Try every recipe in the book. Just once.

The Final Course

Well, my friend, we've done it again. Crawled all the way up to where we can at least jog passably in a brand new world of wonderment. I hope you will scurry off to the produce section of your market just as quickly now as you did when I turned you on to the plant experience.

Just remember—there will be, as there always is in anything new we try—some little valleys on this Green-Brick Road of Cuisinary. But the peaks will more than make up for them, guaranteed!

I am sure, that if you're like I am—and we've pretty much always liked the same things, haven't we?—then you'll eventually settle into a regimen of blended drinks or pancakes or eggs in the morning and maybe a tasty sandwich and some soup or salad for lunch and one of four or five easy and tasty things for dinner. But before you *do* settle into the regimen—try every recipe in the book. Just once. Please.

You'll be doing yourself a favor.

Okay. No time for maudlin sentimentality. We shall meet again, I'm sure, and in the meantime, Happy Growing and Bon Appetit!!

Or as my grandmother used to say—"Enjoy, enjoy!"

Index

INDEX

INDEX